KREŠIMIR ŠEGO • TIME OF GRACE

ZIRAL
THE WOUNDED SWAN PUBLICATIONS
Regular editions
Book 75

Editor-in-Chief
Vinko D. Lasić

Director:
Ivan Tolj

Translated into English and desk-top by
Jozo Kraljević

Printed by
HERCEGTISAK, Široki Brijeg

CIP – Katalogizacija u publikaciji
Nacionalna i sveučilišna knjižnica, Zagreb

UDK 232.931(047.53)

ŠEGO, Krešimir
   Time of Grace / Krešimir Šego ;
[Translated into English by Jozo Kraljević].
– Mostar : Ziral ; Zagreb : K. Krešimir,
1996. – 120 str. ; 18 cm
Prijevod djela: Vrijeme milosti.

ISBN 953-6264-27-7 (Zagreb)
960607073

ISBN 953-6264-27-7

KREŠIMIR ŠEGO

TIME OF
GRACE

Fifteen years of apparitions of the Queen of
Peace in Međugorje
Interviews with Vicka Ivanković and Dr. Fr.
Slavko Barbarić

ZIRAL
MOSTAR, 1996.

Vicka and Fr. Slavko on the March of Peace

PREFACE

From its very beginning Međugorje has had the reputation as a challenge to man's spirit and heart in all its dimensions. There is no area of human spirit or intellect that has not tried its hand at Međugorje, that has not been inspired or affected by the Bijakovići Međugorje events, and we know how it all began.

An attempt to present those beginnings and the subsequent events through a direct conversation after the fifteen-year history and duration of this world-wide phenomenon within the Catholic Church is contained in the book you now have before you. Everything began when some teenagers from Bijakovići first claimed and then until collapse persisted in proving that Our Lady, Mother of God, was appearing to them as the *Queen of Peace* in a time of turmoil and unrest. It required a great deal of daring, courage, and *"disconnectedness" (freakishness)*, if you like, to abide by that claim, for we know quite well in what circumstances the whole thing started to develop, continued and survived. Internal and external circumstances were almost impossible. The physical, moral, psychical pressures were so unbearable that one could objectively doubt the good intentions, subjective conviction and persuasion, as well as the subsequent effects of what had begun in the Church, the world and in the Croatian people on that significant day of June 24, 1981.

Human eyes cannot see, nor can human intellect grasp what an earthquake the appearance of Međugorje on the stage of the world and of the Church caused in the history of the Croatian people themselves, in the revaluation of their history and of their image in the mind of so many who had met the Croatian Catholic being just here in Međugorje or through the Bijakovići visionaries and pastoral workers from the Herzegovinian Franciscan Province who wholeheartedly accepted, spread and are still spreading the messages of Međugorje. Everything that has been happening and is still taking place in these two Herzegovina villages of Bijakovići and Međugorje, these two villages in Herzegovina, followed by the message that set out from there and went around the world, is nothing else but a re-reading of biblical history on the screen of our times and of the biblical word of God in a modern edition that is capable of quenching the thirst and satisfying the hunger of modern man.

Just as we will not find in nature 100% pure water that is capable of quenching man's thirst (distilled water is insipid, tasteless!), so we will likewise not find a 100% pure distilled word of God, but rather a word diffracted through the prism of human experience, vocabulary, intellectual faculties, personal shortcomings, weaknesses, omissions, falls and even sins. For water to be able to quench man's thirst, it must go through earth, sometimes very sullied and soiled, sandy and rocky, through minerals and stones in order to become drinkable in the end. Likewise, God's word ′ too, and in Međugorje it is Our Lady's message, passes through human limitations, and we have it before us in all its simplicity and acceptability, sometimes in its acerbity and bitterness. Just like many medicinal waters taste bitter, but are healing for the organism.

Here the visionaries are children of their age, generation, people, environment and parents. When we look at them in their appearance, we inadvertently think of what St Paul wrote, who *is a fool on Christ's account, who is weak and without honour, who suffers persecution, is slandered on His account, but bears everything patiently and promotes the glad tidings, all on Christ's account.* It almost reaches the limits of human capabilities what, for example, a Vicka, an original witness of the Bijakovići-Međugorje events, *absolves* (and that is exactly what the words ab-solve and absolute contain in their root meaning: dis-solved, dis-connected) in her meetings with pilgrims. She almost no longer belongs to her own self, but she gives herself wholly away, with her heart and being, with all her appearance. The only ones capable of that are the totally committed and witnesses, enraptured till the end, enthusiasts who become martyrs of their conviction and victims of their mission.

Every idea, thought, movement has its rise, enthusiastic acceptance, but also its fatigue, discouragement, its obviously human elements. Father

Slavko – in word, deed and writing – bears witness to the course through Our Lady's school, raises a prophetic voice in the name of God and man, in the name of truth of Our Lady's presence and of the modern man who, without God, verges on the abyss of ruin. By reading his answers we become witnesses of a process that can be followed in the Old Testament, of powerful prophetic criticism of life and practice, especially of practising the faith or lapsing into unbelief. We shall find the same thing in the Gospels, especially in Paul's letters or in prophetic warnings of the Book of Revelation. Neither can Fr. Slavko cease wondering at how some people are ready to sell their mission and birthright for a dish of lentil stew. He is amazed like St Paul, who upbraids his people for *being so stupid: after beginning enthusiastically, in the Spirit, they are now to end in flesh, so it seems they have had such remarkable experiences, have seen so many signs, all to no purpose.* In the first days they chose Our Lady's road, chose God – actually it was God and Our Lady who chose the parish and the parishioners – but now they resort to powerless and worthless forces of this world. They used to receive pilgrims like angels of God, not even knowing that in doing so they were receiving Jesus and Our Lady themselves. That is why Fr. Slavko wonders with St Paul with good reason: *What has happened to your former bliss, to your first love and rapture? I can testify that, if it were possible, you would have plucked out your eyes and given them to Our Lady.* He goes on wondering: *Has she become your enemy just because she tells you the truth, putting it into the ears and before the eyes of you all, you children of Our Lady, to whom she would like to give birth again until Christ is formed in all?* And so one could go on endlessly giving the examples of really instructive and vital parts of the New Testament which are far from mere theory; they rather affect the life practice here in Međugorje and Bijakovići, too. If a man, on the basis of errors of the church people, were to deny the authenticity of Jesus Christ, of the Gospel and of the Divine Revelation, then he would be mixing up the purely divine with the purely human. The divine displays itself in the human weakness and passes through our tight filters, but It cannot be measured by human standards. Fr. Slavko is experienced and wise enough to find a confirmation for his words in Paul who says: *Those who want to be rich are falling into temptation and a trap. They are letting themselves be captured by foolish and harmful desires which drag men down to ruin and destruction, for the love of money is the root of all evil. Some men in their passion for it have strayed from their faith, and have come to grief amid great pain.* Only, who is listening to these distant biblical voices on our modern screen today? No age, no generation, has ever refuted this truth of God's word in a single dot.

If the Međugorje apparitions are a remedy, a sign-post for our times, a word of consolation and encouragement, but also of rebuke and censure, then Our Lady's messages are only a reminder of what Christians already know or should know, and the present prophetic admonitions only a *reminder of the former days when* the Bijakovići or the Međugorje people and all the people of Brotnjo and the

9

Croatian population of Herzegovina and of the nearby regions, *just enlightened* and faced with the Supernatural, *sustained frequent struggles, adversities and sufferings, becoming fellow sufferers; had compassion with captives and joyfully bore every deprivation.* Hence the call: *Let us not give up our meetings,* let us not miss Holy Masses, *but let us encourage each other, for it is really impossible to repeatedly convert those who had been enlightened once, who had tasted the heavenly gift and who had become partakers of the Holy Spirit, who had tasted the good and sweet word of God and the powers of the future world by the strength of Our Lady's appearances and then drew back. Such people are again crucifying the Son of God and making a mockery of Him.* Therefore, Mary's apparitions and her messages are a call back to *the first love and conversion, for it is a fearful thing to fall into the hands of the living God.* Mary, like an angel carrying in her hand *the eternal Gospel,* is calling us all to *the Gospel of Peace and into the service of Jesus in the Holy Spirit.*

Dr. Fr. Tomislav Pervan

(The texts in italics are mainly original or interpreted quotations from the Scriptures.)

AN INTERVIEW
WITH VICKA IVANKOVIĆ

VISIONARIES – BEARERS OF MESSAGES

— Vicka, will you please describe what the feeling of a person is that has been meeting with the Mother of God every day now for fifteen years?

This feeling cannot possibly be put in words, for there are no words to describe it. It is something special, a special peace, satisfaction, a joy that cannot be experienced with any man, but only with Our Lady.

— Are you and the other visionaries different from the others in your same age group?

I cannot see that we are any different from the others in our same age group. We have been called to be different, yet we also try to be like others. But the important thing is that we are spread Our Lady's messages because Our Lady has chosen us. We have nothing specially different from other people, but we do have the responsibility to carry out what Our Lady tells.

— Why were you and the group of children from your neighbourhood chosen to convey Our Lady's messages? Have you ever put this question to yourself, or have you talked about that with the Mother of God?

I could have never dreamt of that. We did ask her once why she had chosen us and she said it had been God's will, not hers.

— Tell us what the Queen of Peace wanted of the visionaries and whether what she wanted has been achieved ?

Our Lady wants us to be actually the bearers of her messages. I can personally say of myself that I really try to accomplish this mission Our Lady asks of me.

— And what did she want of the people?

Our Lady's main messages are that people accept prayer, conversion, fasting, penance and peace. This is what we should accept and live, that is what she wants of us.

— Will you describe to us, by what you have learnt from the meetings with Our Lady, what a Christian should be like today, what the Mother of God expects?

Our Lady does not expect anything special. She says she is not here to bring new messages, to tell us something new, rather she is here to wake us up, for we had fallen asleep and got away from her message.

So, there is nothing new in all that. We only ought to renew the words of the Scriptures and live by them.

— Is the man of today moving towards such a description of a Christian, or is he getting away from it?

Well, It could be said that he's going toward it, but it could still be much better.

MESSAGES

— Will you please repeat the main messages that the Queen of Peace said fifteen years ago and that are still being repeated today?

I think I have already mentioned these messages, but, here, I shall repeat them once again, for there's never enough repetition of Our Lady's messages. Our Lady's main messages are prayer, conversion, fasting, penance and peace. When Our Lady tells us to pray, she is not asking us to pray only with words. She wants us to open our hearts day after day so that prayer might be a real joy for us. Our Lady explained this by a wonderful example. She says: "You all have a flower-pot in your families. If you put two or three drops of water into the pot every day, you will see the flower growing, developing, and there is a beautiful rose in the end." The same happens with our heart. If we put two or three words of prayer into our heart every day, it will grow and develop like that flower does. But if we fail to give water to the flower for two days or so, we shall see it disappearing as if it had never been there. Our Lady says that we, too, many times, when prayer time comes, say: I do not feel like praying today, I am tired, I will do it tomorrow, and so tomorrow comes and the day after tomorrow... That way every day we get ourselves farther away from prayer and everything that comes from that bad side starts to enter into our heart. For Our Lady says: "As a flower cannot live without water, so we cannot live without God's grace. For the prayer of the heart can never be learnt; the prayer of the heart can only be lived, by making one step forward day after day."

When Our Lady recommends fasting, she is not asking the sick to fast on bread and water, but to give up something they like best; while the persons who are healthy but say they cannot fast because they get a headache or dizziness, lack strong will. Our Lady says, if we fast out of love for Jesus and herself then there will be no problems, for all that we lack is strong will. When Our Lady says "peace", she herself came here and said: "I am the Queen of Peace and have come to bring peace." But she has not come only to bring peace to the world; she came first of all to bring peace into our hearts, into our families. And only when we have that peace, can we pray for peace in the world. For if we pray for peace in the world, but have no personal peace in our heart, such prayer is not worth much.

Furthermore, Our Lady calls us to complete conversion. Our Lady says that when we are in problems, difficulties, in troubles, we always think that she and Jesus are far from us but that is not true. Our Lady and Jesus are always by our side. We should open our hearts in order to understand how much Our Lady loves us.

Likewise, Our Lady points out in a special way to put Holy Mass in the first place and that it is the most important and the most sacred moment, for it is the living Jesus who comes at that moment and we receive Him into our hearts. Through all that time we prepare ourselves in a special way so that we could receive Jesus with love and in the most worthy manner possible.

Our Lady then recommends that we go to confession once a month, and also, she says, as the need may arise, as an individual may feel. We must not take confession as something routine: just go and get rid of sins and then continue living as before, but we must change and become new persons asking advice from the priest how to make a step forward.

— Does Our Lady talk with you about the fruits of the apparitions, the fruits of her messages?

Certainly, she does. She says there are enough fruits but again it depends on us, on how much we are ready to pick Our Lady's messages. For Our Lady does nothing by force. It is all our will, for God gave us all freedom.

Our Lady has not come to force one to believe, to tell him or her: "You shall believe, you must believe!" He who wants to believe, believes; he who does not, is free to do so.

— From the messages that Our Lady gives monthly through Marija I can see that she sometimes says, "I am happy" and sometimes, "I am sad". What most of all makes her happy or again most of all makes her unhappy?

I cannot comment on the message that Our Lady gives every 25th in the month, because she does not tell it to me but to Marija. When Our Lady tells a message to me, I am able to explain it to you, but when I hear it from Marija, I hear it like all others.

Our Lady is most happy when we accept her message, and our blasphemies make her unhappy, that is, not accepting the messages.

— What is the main reason that the effects of Our Lady's messages are not felt more strongly, so that people accept them with difficulty?

That depends most of all on the person. We should try to pray for the grace from Jesus and Our Lady to help us, naturally along with our good will, to open our hearts. If we "manage" to open them, there will be no problems accepting Our Lady's message.

Our Lady once said that people are afraid of changing their life, because at that moment they might be feeling well and think, if they accept the message, who knows what lies in store for them. I say they have nothing to be afraid of, for they have not been at ease so far anyway.

If we are not ready to open our heart and surrender ourselves to God's love, then we shall be in fear all our life and shall never be free.

— Family life is the mainstay for a healthy Christian life. Which of Our Lady's messages would be crucial for achieving Christian life in a family?

Our Lady says she would be especially happy if the prayer of the rosary were renewed in our families. Parents ought to pray with the children, and the children with the parents, so that Satan may not be able to do us any harm. Lately Our Lady has been especially pointing out how strong Satan is. Satan wants to hamper us in everything: in our peace, in our families. That is why Our Lady wants us to pray the rosary, and that is the mightiest weapon against Satan. Only in this way, through prayer, sharing, conversation, and Bible reading, can a family of today hold out.

It is usually up to the parents to start praying in the families, but nowadays, unfortunately, it is the children who seem to be starting first, not the parents. But for Our Lady it is not important who it will be, it is important to start. If there is somebody in the family who opposes it, one should not force him, one should leave it to his will. We are here to help him with our way of life and example, so that our prayer might find its way to his heart and that he may come to know the joy of it.

So we have to be patient, for we cannot achieve anything by shouting and cursing. All we can do is to bring it home to him by our example that he, too, ought to change.

– Young people are exposed to many pitfalls today. What should be done essentially in order to protect youth from these dangers? I mean, there are young people who have already got into huge problems, for example with drugs, and who are being cured, but what about those who have no opportunity to be treated, for example, against drugs?

Yes. But the main problem is not that these unhappy boys and girls have no opportunity for treatment. The main problem is that such young people, although addicted, will not admit to themselves or to others that they are needy of help. You see, here in Međugorje we have one such community where the young are being cured from drug addiction, and I know these boys are not ashamed of openly talking about their life. They lead prayers, go around schools and give lectures on addiction. But today's parents are ashamed to admit they have an addict in the family, they will not admit it to themselves and will not talk about it with the children. Today the parents are afraid of coming closer to their child.

It is not all right for the parents to say to their children, "Here, take this or that much money, go wherever you want and do whatever you please!" and I think it is exactly here that the root of this ruin lies. And today, in these times, just in these areas of Međugorje, Bijakovići and Čitluk and other places, people have the chance of making money, but it is exactly with money that most evils come. For if people themselves are not able to distinguish between good and evil, and are not asking for a special blessing, they will end up in sin.

Our Lady says herself that the young are in a very difficult situation at the moment and says she is worried herself. We can only help them with our prayer and love.

— How should we approach young people and urge them to start thinking themselves more seriously about that?

The young need guidance today. I know for sure

that priests can do very much in this respect, and if they can't, nobody else can. This is the moment when something should be done indeed. I often get disappointed when talking to young people: they rarely look into your eyes. Their eyes are void of joy. I try to make them smile a bit, but there is no response, they look completely uninterested, as if they lacked will for life.

APPARITIONS

— Tell me what impressed you most about Our Lady.

Well, I couldn't say anything special. Each time the meeting with Our Lady makes me marvel so much as if it were the first time. I never ask for anything special. But speaking about the details, I can say that it is magnificent to see Our Lady for Christmas when she appears with baby Jesus in her arms. Two years ago she came with the "big" Jesus on Good Friday. He was in wounds all over, in torn clothes and with a crown of thorns on the head. Our Lady says, "I have come for you to see how much Jesus suffered for you", and so we saw Him both when he was a baby and at the moment of his passion, of his death. Well, I point this out because it refers to Jesus, but as for Our Lady, I couldn't single out anything, for all her appearance is simply magnificent.

— Will you describe to us the appearance, the figure, the disposition of the Queen of Peace the way you see and experience her?

Each time before Our Lady comes, we see a light

three times, which is a sign that she is coming. When she appears, she has a white veil, a crown of stars on her head, her eyes are blue, the hair black, the cheeks rosy; she is hovering in the air on a grey cloud, so she does not touch the ground. For some greater festivities, for example Christmas and Easter, or for her birthday, she wears a robe of gold.

— Is she a woman from the distant past or is she a woman of our times?

I personally experience her a person from our times, therefore, as though she were living at this time.

— Have people responded to Our Lady's messages, to her calls to conversion, prayer and penance?

Once Our Lady said that there are a lot of people who accept a message, start living it and then they sort of get tired. But she would much prefer, she says, if we accepted a message with the heart and went a step forward without stopping. People accept everything all at once and then stop all at once.

We should accept the messages gradually, start living them and pray, and then we shall not become tired, if we, of course, accept them with the heart. This is a bit more difficult to explain to people. If Our Lady says at this moment, "Pray three rosaries", she does not mean that we should recite three rosaries the same moment. She first said, "Pray at least seven Our Fathers", after seven Our Fathers she said, "Pray joyful mysteries", but no hurry: today we shall do one mystery, tomorrow another, or today we shall live one Our Father, tomorrow another, etc. Then after half a year she said, "Pray sorrowful mysteries", and in a year we shall pray glorious ones, etc. So, nothing was sudden. At this moment it may seem too much to people, but at that moment it was not much, everything was gradual. Today, when I convey Our Lady's message, that is after fifteen years, I can't say, "You pray a decade today", for I am obliged to report fully what Our Lady says.

— Do we know how to hear the messages, are we changing?

We know very well how to hear and understand the message quite well. The trouble is that we resort to the messages mostly when we have some problem, but you see, God even uses that way so He can draw people closer to Himself.

— You mean that, through the apparitions of the Blessed Virgin Mary, people are after all growing in faith, that fruits are visible?

Of course. Our Lady says herself that faith is a great gift, and if we want this gift to grow in our heart we have to pray to God daily. For it is not difficult to say, "I believe", for it is only words. A man has to show by his deeds what and how strong he believes.

During her second apparition Our Lady said she was the Queen of Peace. One of the main messages, of the main calls upon people, was the call to peace. How did you, as a young lady then, experience that call to peace, did you understand it, since there was no war here or in Europe at that time?

May I correct you on this point? Namely, at her second apparition Our Lady said, "I am the Blessed Virgin Mary", and a few days later she said, "I am the Queen of Peace and I have come to bring peace". Yes, I myself was puzzled why Our Lady should say, "I have come to bring you peace". For it was rather peaceful in Europe then, and I could not really understand what she meant by that. But Our Lady kept repeating through her messages, "Pray for peace", "Through prayer and fasting even wars may be warded off", etc. We did sometimes hear of wars in Iran and Iraq, but we hardly knew where that was until finally one day this war of ours occurred.

Our Lady said she had been among us for ten full years giving us messages to help her prevent this war, but we failed to respond to her call.

— **In the present meetings what does Our Lady say about peace or war?**

At the moment Our Lady is speaking mostly about the family and young people who are, as I have already said, in a very difficult situation today. She is calling us to peace, too, but to peace of mind, a peace that people are supposed to find by the spirit. Presently, she isn't saying anything about wars.

OUR LADY LOVES US ALL EQUALLY

— **In 1981 mankind was divided in two opposing halves in regard to a life of faith. Namely, in Communism faith was forbidden and undesirable, so**

24

that in many countries few people were practising their faith. In the free non-communist world faith was not practised much either for conformist reasons; people bent on material goods crave after them ever more, getting away from God more and more. The apparitions in Međugorje were a call to both to come back to God, to get free?

Our Lady says, "I am the Mother of all people", and she loves us all equally. She does not make distinction between men, that is she does not divide them. It was rather men who made such divisions so that these men have got very far from each other, meaning, first of all, nations, peoples, or origins. But we are all equal before God, for God is one for all. Well, let us take me as an example: I have visions, that is, I speak with Our Lady, but it does not mean she loves me more than others; I personally think she loves us all alike, the only difference being that I have the favour of conversing with Our Lady.

— You got to know the Blessed Virgin Mary, God's wishes and demands on us most directly. How, from your experience, do you view the return to God, that is, are men returning to God?

Yes, men are returning to God, and this can lately be seen most clearly by Our Lady's look, for it can really be noticed that she is much happier. But again, on the other side, they are not returning in the number Our Lady would expect and wish.

— The Queen of Peace always addresses us with gentleness, even when reprimanding us. However, in this gentleness of a Mother the demands are very strict – strict in terms of conversion, prayer, fasting. In one word, she demands self-denial. How do you see a life of faith?

I couldn't say Our Lady reprimands us, at least not in the true sense of the word. Our Lady always has a smile on her face, but many times I felt she was sad. When she appears, I can always tell whether she is happy or unhappy. She always has mild eyes, and I have never had a feeling that she might be reprimanding us. Her reprimand is maybe her very love, her cherishing us so much.

— Often, when you are having a vision, many people are present. How does Our Lady look upon a sinner or, for example, upon you?

In Our Lady's eyes there is no difference between me or a sinner, as you say. Our Lady hopes that a sinner will better himself, will convert. She may love him even more for that, and offer him more love than to me, for she wants to save him and release him from sin.

— What charms you most in the apparitions, what fascinates and enchants you most?

Maybe the feeling as if you were no more on earth, as if you were suspended in the air.

— From the very beginning of the apparitions the visionaries have been in a privileged position for us ordinary believers. You have been initiated into many secrets, you have been shown paradise, hell and purgatory. Vicka, what is it like to live with

the secrets that have been confided to you by the Mother of God?

So far Our Lady has given me nine out of ten possible secrets. That is no burden for me, for when she gave me the secrets, she also gave me the strength to cope with them. I live as if I did not have them at all.

— Do you know when the tenth secret will be imparted?

No, I don't.

— Do you think about the secrets, is it difficult to bear them, are they something of a burden to you?

Yes, I certainly think about them, for the secrets contain the future, but I am not burdened with it.

— Do you know when the secrets will be available to people?

No, I don't know that either.

— Our Lady has narrated her biography to you. Can you say anything about her life now? When will that be available?

Our Lady has told me all her biography, from birth till Assumption. I could not say anything about it at the moment, for I have no authorisation to do so. Our Lady's whole lifetime is contained in three notebooks in which I was putting down what Our Lady was telling me. Sometimes I would write one page, another time two, sometimes only half a page, depending on how much I was able to remember.

MEETINGS WITH PILGRIMS

— When speaking of the fruits of the apparitions of the Queen of Peace in the parish of Međugorje, looking superficially, it seems as if nothing had changed. Men are still far away from God, but when we consider how many have come to the shrine of the Queen of Peace – millions – how many have been converted, the world is much more different in 1996 than it used to be in 1981, both in our people and in the world. What are, in your opinion, the most important fruits of the apparitions?

I have already told you, the most important fruit of the apparitions is the acceptance of her message. Our Lady wants us to be the bearers of her message, to change our hearts.

— You are always, every day, in front of your house in Podbrdo, praying with the pilgrims and talking friendly, with a smile. If you are not at home, then you are in countries all over the world. Vicka, what is it that interests pilgrims most in the meetings with visionaries, with you, for example?

Every morning, in wintertime, I start working with people about nine o'clock, or at eight in summertime, so that I could talk to as many people as possible. People come with various problems and wishes, and I try to help them as much as I can. I take pains to hear each of them out and say a few good words. I make efforts to find some time for everybody, but sometimes it is simply impossible so that I myself feel sometimes sorry, for I think I could have done more. However, I have noticed lately that people ask less and less questions. For example, I received recently a group of about a thousand people: Americans, Poles, about five buses of Checks and Slovaks, etc. But it is interesting that nobody asked me anything.

It is enough for them that I pray over them and say a few words to make them happy.

— Are there those who would like to speak to you in private, and what do they expect from you?

Yes, of course, there are, and I believe that every man has a problem that bothers him and that he would like to get rid of. People expect from me to be open in the first place, to convey Our Lady's message to them and to give them hope. I repeat, I try as much as I can, and I can tell by their look that they are satisfied after the talk with me.

— What does a typical meeting of yours with the pilgrims look like?

For example, I get up at eight o'clock in the morning, when I have a meeting with Italian pilgrims. Of course, first I tell them Our Lady's message, after that they have a meeting with Mirjana at nine o'clock. Afterwards I have a meeting with English and American pilgrims. I would like to stress that the Americans always want me to bless them, which I always do. The talk with them takes about an hour or so, depending on the number of pilgrims, and they are followed by the Brazilians, etc. In general, the day passes in talks and prayer.

– You travel a lot. Which countries have you visited?

I have visited many countries. I have been to Canada, several times to the United States, to Brazil, and I have also visited most European countries. Sister Elvira, leader of the community for the treatment of drug addicts, who is here in Međugorje, has opened a new sanatorium in Brazil, near Sao Paolo, and so we are about to visit this place. On our way there we would first visit Florida, where there are such communities, too.

— I was with you on a praying tour, and I am happy about that, and I saw how delighted the people were at meeting with you. At such meetings people experience Međugorje in a concentrated prayer. What do people most often expect from such meetings and what do you recommend to them?

People, for sure, expect a lot sometimes, but I am always the same. What I offered in one place I shall offer in another, too. It is mainly the people who have never been to Međugorje, and all that is new for them, so that they expect a lot from such meetings. I manage to do much of what they expect. I have a programme by which I work and which is mainly made according to their wishes.

— How do you personally feel at such prayer meetings? Tell us something about your most important ones.

I always look forward to such meetings, and each meeting is special to me, but I would single out the meeting with an Indian tribe in Canada. We visited their wigwams, attended the Holy Mass together with them, and I was very much impressed by the meeting with their priest and by the respect they received us with. For Communion they all lined up and took Communion, which surprised me very much. There followed the Adoration, and then they prepared various traditional festivities, too, which was magnificent for me indeed. And it all was happening in the open air, under a cross.

Everything happens under that cross with great mental concentration, no matter if it's rainy or windy.

— **Had they known anything about the apparitions in Međugorje before your coming?**

Yes, they had, but nobody had visited it before. Father Slavko had also met Indians elsewhere but he had not been in those parts. Father Svetozar and I visited that place at the suggestion of the organiser. To the question whether we should visit the Indians, too, I said we would rather shorten one of our programmes and go to them.

In prayer meetings there is no difference for me whether it is this or that, whether it is a rich man or a poor man. We are all the same; there are neither rich nor poor; what matters most is that a man is rich in spirit. I have never taken account of whether one is rich or poor. For me a rich man is the one who is rich in spirit, but should one have something else besides, thank God, it was God who blessed him with that. Conversion is a grace.

— **How much effort is needed to start conversion and a life in accordance with the messages?**

It does not require much effort. What matters

most is that you want conversion. If you want conversion, it will come, and no effort is needed at all. But as long as you struggle, as long as there is a fight going on inside you, it means you are not determined to make that step. You'd better never start struggling if you are not persistent to the end, asking of God the favour of conversion.

Conversion is a grace, conversion will not drop down out of the blue sky, if you do not want it. Our conversion is our whole life. Who can say today, "I am converted"? Nobody. We have to go the way of conversion. Whoever says he is converted is lying, he hasn't moved an inch. He who says he wants to be converted, he is on the way of conversion, he prays for conversion every day.

— Apart from the meetings with pilgrims in our parish and prayer meetings, you also keep in touch with a lot of people from the world. What do such contacts mean to these people?

I keep mail and telephone contacts. Usually, people who cannot come call me by phone, they want to recommend themselves, to pray; the people who are at hospital, who are dying, want to hear a word of consolation, of hope. They are aware of their condition, they want to recommend themselves, to pray one Our Father, or Hail Mary, with me on the phone. At any time, I accept such talks, for I know what they mean to such people. They feel as if they were in Medugorje, they are relieved.

I cannot reply to every letter received, for it would hardly leave me any time for anything else. But where I see that it is urgent, where it is necessary, I do reply to such letters. I beg the people not to be angry when they do not get an answer to their letter, for I could be replying day and night. To those who send their letters through pilgrims, I reply with a few words, such as, "I pray for you", "I greet you", or the like, so that they may know I have received and read the letter.

— Are you personally satisfied with the acceptance of the messages?

On the one hand, I am satisfied, on the other hand I am not. People accept and don't accept the messages. I wouldn't like to condemn anybody for not accepting the messages, or say that the messages are being accepted slowly. I don't look upon it from the standpoint that I might condemn one, far from it. I look upon it this way: As much as I could do more, so much more could other people do. Nobody should be condemned or blamed. If I, as a visionary, think I can and should do more, so everyone should think: It's high time I moved at least an inch.

— Other apparitions lasted briefly, for a few days, while in Međugorje they have been going on for fifteen years now?

Yes. Once when we asked Our Lady how long she was going to stay, she replied, "Have you become bored with me?" Then we decided not to ask her again. Let it last as long as it will. Our Lady said she would finish here in Međugorje what she had started in Fatima. She gave this in a message.

— You, Ivan, Marija and Jakov have visions on a

daily basis, and Mirjana and Ivanka only occasionally?

Yes, the four of us have a vision every day. For her birthday on March 18 Mirjana had a vision, and Ivanka will have a vision for the anniversary. Two of them once a year, and we every day.

— How do you feel during an apparition? Has anything changed in comparison with the first days of apparitions?

Nothing has changed. To me the meeting is somehow always the same. You prepare yourself through prayer, and so the prayer builds up every meeting that comes. The more you pray, the more you prepare yourself, the more prepared you get for the meeting.

— What does an apparition look like? Will you describe it to us?

The apparition takes place always at the same time: at twenty to six in the wintertime, or at twenty to seven in the summertime. Here there is nothing special. Other people are also present during an apparition. The rosary is recited, sometimes one, another time two decades, so that the meeting happens through prayer indeed. I usually convey people's recommendations, or recommend somebody personally. (If there is some special question, I put it, await Our Lady's message, what she is going to say.) There is no suspense at the apparitions, but at each meeting you feel different, for each day is a new day. I often say to the Blessed Virgin Mary, "Our Lady, you know that I am eager to help people", then I pray with Our Lady for the needy.

— **How do you talk with Our Lady? Is it a free conversation?**

The same as with you now, quite free, there is no difference.

— **Have you talked about the future of the apparitions?**

No, I haven't. She will tell it herself. When it comes to important questions, Our Lady will tell herself, so that I don't ask it.

ON THE HILL OF APPARITIONS OUR LADY WILL LEAVE A PERMANENT, VISIBLE AND INDESTRUCTIBLE SIGN

— **In the fist days of apparitions you and other visionaries were talking about a sign Our Lady was going to leave, a visible sign. Has anything changed about the sign, will it be given indeed?**

Yes, it will. Nothing has changed. It is the third secret Our Lady gave. She will leave a sign on the apparition spot. The sign will be permanent, visible and indestructible, it will remain forever.

— **You know what kind of a sign is that?**

Yes, we saw it once.

— **In the first days, months and years of apparitions a lot of people were expecting some kind of a sign, a miracle, something extraordinary. Later on this seemed to be disappearing, and people prayed more, worked on their inner transformation. Is it so, and what do you have to say about that?**

That's right. There are a lot of people who, when they come, say they see the sun spinning, they see some changes on Mt. Križevac, they say their rosaries changed colour. Our Lady says these are only small tokens, but it is most important that we change inside, that we change our heart. If you are given such a sign, it means it's time for you to start changing, and not to attach so much importance to it. It is important to change inside, but if you are given such a sign, then you must know that it was given because you should do something.

— **There have been some miraculous healings. Will you say something more about it?**

Yes. But the parish office could give you a better answer for they have all the evidence of healings. The healed come to me after the event to say hello and give thanks, but I don't keep records on that, that's what the parish office does.

— **How is it possible to bring the rhythm, the speed of today's way of life, into accord with the requests of Our Lady's messages?**

Nowadays we live very fast and we have to slow down. If we go on at such speed, go on living like this, we shall get nowhere. We should never say, "I have to, I have to". God's will is in everything, there's time for everything. The problem is in us. We are the ones who dictate the rhythm. If we say to ourselves, "Easy!" then the world will change, too. It is up to us, it's no fault of God, but ours. We imposed the speed on ourselves and assumed that we can't do without it.

That way we are not free, and we are not free

36

because we don't want to be free. If you yourself want to be free, you will find the way to be so.

— Which prayers does the Queen of Peace recommend most?

Above all she recommends the rosary. That is her favourite prayer: joyful, sorrowful and glorious mysteries. Every prayer, Our Lady says, which comes from the heart, which is said with love, is good.

— And the Creed, seven Our Fathers, Hail Marys and Glory Bes?

That was the minimum. Later, after I had already been repeating these prayers for some time, she said, "We shall pray the rosary", but, she says, it is important to meditate on every word you utter. It's no use taking the rosary beads into the hands now, reciting three mysteries, if you remain as empty as before, maybe even emptier. Nothing will come of it. To say one Hail Mary, but so that it remains in your heart, avails more than your having said all the three rosaries without meditating.

— The fifteenth year of apparitions is coming to its close. How much, in your opinion, has been realised of what the Blessed Virgin Mary has been recommending by her coming to Međugorje?

I think that a lot has been realised. I can tell it by her look. But again, much more could have been done if we had been a bit different. A lot has been realised, Our Lady is not dissatisfied.

— What is Our Lady expecting from us now?

At his moment? She is expecting what she has been expecting since the beginning. There are still people who are only starting, but there are also people who are going forward, so that Our Lady is expecting the same.

— **Are you in the position to discuss the future of the shrine?**

I really can't say anything. It would be of no avail. For what I would project, would be my own making, but Our Lady knows what she wants. Our Lady will be announcing little by little what should be, so I am not worried at all, nor am I encumbered by that. I know that Our Lady is in control of everything.

— **You practically don't have a private life. You are always at the disposal of pilgrims and the sick, you take part in prayer meetings... Do you ever become tired of it?**

No, it doesn't bother me. It is God's grace and God's will. I never become tired a bit. I often say, if one wants and wishes to do something, to be at Our Lady's service and do what she asks, he will never become tired of it. I often say, I can't manage everything the way I would like it, but at least I try as much as I can.

— **Your prayer, meetings with people, with pilgrims, and all you are doing, you do with your familiar, constant smile. Do you ever get angry?**

I don't know. There's no need or reason for anger. I don't know why one should get angry. No matter what one might say to me, I am not angry, I receive everybody without anger. Maybe it's a special grace, or I am such character, I don't know... It never occurs to me, the anger. I have no time to be angry.

ALL MEN ARE OUR LADY'S CHILDREN

— What do you recommend to the people in our parish and to pilgrims?

I don't recommend anything myself, anything out of my own head. I recommend Our Lady's message, and nothing of my own making. Always when I talk to somebody, I point out what is *my* advice, I warn him that it is mine, not Our Lady's, just to avoid every misunderstanding. What Our Lady says, I point out. Nevertheless, people often convey that wrongly. I have no need to present what is mine if I have what is more important, what we all are told.

— The messages that Our Lady gives on every 25th in the month always start with "Dear children". Who are her children, the visionaries or all men?

All. All of us who are willing to accept her message. We are all her children. When she gives us a message, she gives it for the whole world, for everybody who wants to be Our Lady's child.

We, the visionaries, have our faults, for sure, nobody is perfect. What matters most is that a man wants to change, to go forward, to help others. The most important thing is to live Our Lady's message. If I am not ready to live it, why should I tell it to others? If you want to live Our Lady's message,

39

if you want to change, if you build it up in your heart, then you may tell it to others, too. As long as you do not undertake anything, you'd better keep silent.

— Your family is burdened, too?

Yes, but they have accepted it. God gave them that gift and I really think they are bearing it all right. I have a wonderful family. They know what is mine, they know that every morning I have meetings with pilgrim groups. When I finish with it, I am at their disposal. As for my family, there is nothing that might obstruct my obligations towards the pilgrims.

— Do you ever get tired of so many obligations, of so many people?

I don't feel a bit tired. Never. My work always starts early in the morning and lasts until far into the night. Every day.

— You are often with the sick. What are your experiences?

There *are* sick people. But those sick in spirit are more seriously ill than the physically sick. People need a word of consolation, they only ask for strength. It is hard to say today that sickness is a great gift of God, it's unimaginable telling a sick person, who suffers of cancer, for example, or of any other disease, that it is a gift of God. Everybody tries to get rid of a disease. Far be it from him.

But, indeed, Our Lady says that sickness is a gift of God, for God knows why He has given this gift to me, to you, to anybody, and He knows when he will take it back, and He demands our patience. Nothing has been given without a reason; everything has its why, and so, she says, when it is given to you, say, "Thank you, O God, for this gift, if you have another such gift I am ready to accept it. But give me also the strength that I may do this for You with the heart and with love". Our Lady once pointed out that we are not able even to imagine what an importance our suffering has in the eyes of God.

— How do seriously ill people feel when you are with them?

The people are glad, for I pray over them, give them a word of consolation, convey them the message. They feel instantly relieved.

— What does Međugorje mean in the world today?

Međugorje means a lot, for sure. I mean not Međugorje as a place, but Međugorje as a message certainly means a lot. It is really something that one cannot imagine, I mean that Our Lady's message has spread all over the world, to its farthest corner. Judging by the messages I receive, by the letters from all over the world, people are delighted. This has become an oasis of peace; nowhere can a man find such a peace as here under Our Lady's shelter, in her presence, covered with her mantle. That's why it is so. But Međugorje is great by Our Lady's message and because Our Lady is still here, because her presence is still on a daily basis. Lourdes, Fatima and other places *are* pilgrim places, it's wonderful to be in them, but one has a different feeling in a place where Our Lady is "alive" than in a place she had been at and gone. That's why people feel that Medugorje is great, because Heaven is still on Earth here, and because Our Lady is present every day.

One cannot compare this to anything, one cannot express in words what Medugorje means. We who live here maybe are not the right persons to make such a judgment. It is so because we have become used to it and cannot put ourselves into the position of one who comes here.

For all people who come, Medugorje is holy ground.

— Since the first days of apparitions you and all other visionaries have been claiming that Our Lady speaks to you in the Croatian language?

Yes, and there is no greater favour than that. But we are not aware of that favour. Our Lady has accepted us, our people, to speak to others through us, but we forget sometimes to say, "Thank you". We do not appreciate enough what has been given to us.

— In the war that has befallen us, Our Lady has protected us?

Our Lady knows, God knows best. God's favour is endless and He forgets no nation. At this moment, in our difficult moments of war and everything, only now do we really see how much Our Lady loves us and how much God loves us. They had foreseen the war and all the destruction and that's why she came to us. It is really a great favour beyond any comparison. We can never thank God

42

enough; as long as one lives, he can never thank enough for this favour. The war came, true, but so did the help from people all over the world. The friends of Međugorje are the friends of the Croatian people, which could be best felt during the war. Our Lady let our people be helped in this way, too.

— **Are you satisfied with the way journalists render your interviews?**

Not even five percent do they convey of what I say. I cannot understand such twisting. I will do everything for the one who spreads Our Lady's message. If needed, I won't sleep for a month, only that good might be done.

— **Even during the most difficult war days Međugorje was not without pilgrims?**

No, it wasn't. During the war the French were the most numerous. Before the war they had been very few, but when the war broke out, they started coming, at times five buses of them would come at once, which impressed me very much indeed. They keep on coming. Today they are among the most numerous pilgrims.

— **Vicka, what do the site of the apparitions, the Hill of Apparitions, Mt. Križevac and the church mean to you?**

The site of the apparitions is the spot Our Lady steps upon, it's there that she comes, that is number one. Križevac on the other hand is a place of penance, the Way of the Cross, a real Calvary. Our Lady comes to us on Mt. Križevac when we go there with a prayer group, that's great. And the

43

church, again, is something special, for Our Lady says Mass is the most important. You climb Podbrdo and Križevac, and then you return to the church and do all that is important during the day, Mass being the crown of everything. Our Lady said, "The presence of God at church is more important than my presence, my being here". Although she is "live" here, Our Lady wants to stress how much more important Jesus' presence is.

— Pilgrims from various countries celebrate Holy Mass here in Međugorje in their languages, English, German, French, Spanish, Italian, Polish, Hungarian, Portuguese, Check, Slovak and other languages. However, a large number of them are present at the evening Mass. What attracts them in such large numbers to a Mass in the Croatian language, which they do not understand?

The evening Mass is a Mass for pilgrims, and for pilgrims it is quite enough to be present at it. Our Lady speaks Croatian, the Mass is in Croatian, Our Lady is present at that Mass. Of course there are no differences between Masses. We can see for ourselves how much the pilgrims are concentrated. Although they do not understand the language, they are profoundly participating in the Mass.

— Do you still have visions on the Hill of Apparitions?

At this moment, no. When we all come together, we have visions both on the Hill of Apparitions and on Križevac, it depends.

44

GOD SHALL FORSAKE NOBODY

— **Our Lady tells you when a vision is going to take place on the Hill of Apparitions or on Kri-**
ževac?

Yes. She tells whether and when it will be, on Podbrdo or on Križevac.

— **Otherwise, you have a vision every day?**

Yes, every day.

— **How long does a vision last?**

Anywhere between five minutes and half an hour, it depends.

— **We have had a war, people have suffered a lot, and now they are worried about the future, about their jobs, about their life. In fact, people all over the world are worried about their jobs, salaries, about their future. There is a general hustle and bustle everywhere. How to bring such a way of life into harmony with what Our Lady asks?**

Man is too much worried and bothered. There is too much fear of loss, but one should not be afraid. God shall never abandon anybody; we here, with our experience of this war, are a proof for that.

Each of us should examine himself, find some time for his family, surrender oneself to God's will, to His guidance. He who strives for material things is a million times poorer than the one who aspires after spiritual wealth.

There is nothing stronger than God's spirit and Our Lady's love. This must be clear to us. If we are seeking that, then our heart swells and all problems disappear. If you gave me the whole world now, I would say no thank you, I don't need it; I am happier with what I have today and nobody can be happier.

For, as long as you are satisfied with what you have, you will go forward, but if you grab, you will lose even what you have got.

— **Abortion is a big problem in the world today. Have you talked with Our Lady about that?**

Once Our Lady told me that the persons who do an abortion commit a grave sin. The children killed that way are little angels for whose death the persons who have done it are responsible .

One should put oneself the question how many people get killed in war, and how many in a mother's bosom. Those killed in war are mourned, but children just conceived as though they were not human. There is no difference whether one is killed in war or in an abortion. The responsibility is equal. But man's conscience seems to have failed completely.

— **The visionaries are the apostles of Our Lady's messages, and so are the priests who have accepted the messages. But the faithful who have accepted them are also their propagators. What should be done about spreading the messages?**

Every man is called upon to spread Our Lady's messages, just as we were chosen by God to convey the message to people. Our Lady says she is glad for every pilgrim who comes to Međugorje, but she is even happier, she says, when they accept the message with the heart, live it themselves, and so spread it to other people through their life and example.

— **Has Our Lady maybe a special message for such people?**

To accept the message is a great grace that Our Lady grants. Whoever has accepted the message, has also been given the gift of spreading it further.

— **At the beginning of the apparitions the visionaries had problems with the authorities. But even nowadays there are those who look with a sneer on the whole thing. Are you embarrassed when you meet such people?**

The other visionaries and I never had problems with the authorities; rather it was the authorities who had problems with us. As concerns our situation, neither I nor any of the visionaries did anything bad, we bothered nobody, but the authorities were bothered. We have always been calm and we used to tell the authorities what I am telling you now or what I have been telling everybody for fifteen years. That they did not want to accept our words is up to them, it's their problem.

The one who looks at the messages and the apparitions with a sneer is making fun of himself, not us. It's a time and a chance for his conversion, too.

— **With her messages in Međugorje Our Lady urges people in many ways to change. What should be done so that people may take a greater part in the acceptance of the message and in the change?**

47

Our Lady is constantly calling us to accept the messages. She often says that we are ready to accept the messages hastily, and then to cool down, to stop living by them. As if people got tired. She would be happier, she says, if we were changing slowly in our heart, in our inner selves. If we say we are ready to change and accept that gift, God will find a way for us to persevere. Then there are no problems. It is essential that we make a decision ourselves.

— You and the other visionaries are at a meeting every day with Our Lady, that is with the other world, with paradise. Can this life be compared with the one that awaits us in the world beyond?

Our Lady says that we on earth can live paradise, hell or purgatory, depending on what a man will decide for. Likewise, she says that here on earth many think that death is the end of everything. Our Lady herself confirmed that we are only sojourners on earth and that never can we compare this world with what awaits us in heaven.

AN INTERVIEW WITH FATHER
SLAVKO BARBARIĆ

IN OUR LADY'S SCHOOL

— We are on the threshold of the 15th anniversary of Our Lady's apparitions in Međugorje. The Queen of Peace has been visiting the Earth day after day, dwelling among us, praying with the visionaries, calling everybody to change their lives, calling for changes within the social community. You have been a firsthand witness of the events, changes, numberless have been your meetings with pilgrims to Međugorje, and you also carry Our Lady's messages all over the world. Consequently, the first question in this interview would be: What has happened in the world in these fifteen years? How do you look at the world then and now, and what has happened in these fifteen years that has filled up this, for an age of man, important time period?

This question is difficult to answer, since the events in the world in these last years have been numerous and very important, and certainly the reasons for changes cannot be simply brought under one common denominator, nor is it possible to find all the reasons for these events so easily.

If we remember the situation in the '80s, or more exactly in 1981, then we can generally say that at that time a very strong Communist structure existed in many European countries, the Berlin wall was still standing firm, "Solidarity" in Poland had tried to initiate some changes. The tension between America and Russia was obvious, the Warsaw Pact was in confrontation with the NATO pact. And the situation in the then Yugoslavia was uncertain, due to Tito's illness and old age. Fifteen years ago one could look on the world in a static way. Everything seemed firm and clear. Today, however, after the disappearance of Communism, all the consequences that remained after it, especially the economic crisis appearing in the free world, corroborate the fact that everything is changing, and that historical changes, so slow and sometimes unexpected, are quite real.

It is difficult and maybe presumptuous to try to explain everything by the appearance of the Medugorje apparitions, but it can be said with certainty that these apparitions and the related events are more and more at the centre of world events and of people's consciousness. Many changes have occurred during the time of Medugorje.

— In 1981, when the visionaries had their first meeting with the Queen of Peace, they were children, the youngest being only 10, and the oldest almost 17. You have been, for almost fifteen years, in daily contact with the children, or rather you have been cooperating with them. What has their growing up been like? What has been happening to the visionaries in terms of their physical and mental growing into adult, mature persons?

The visionaries are the persons that Our Lady

took from among us and made them her messengers. We are all in danger of thinking that they are special persons with special gifts. However, they are, in the strict sense, persons like everyone else. It is difficult to speak of their interior growth, of their maturation in the mental and spiritual sense, because they are all different. Besides, in no way are we able to conclude what they would have been like if on that day, June 24, 1981, they had not become visionaries. It is an irrefutable fact that, in spite of all the difficulties, each of them has remained consistent with what he or she has been testifying: I am seeing Our Lady and she calls us all to peace. This does not, at first sight, speak so much of them as persons, as believers and so on, as it does of Mary with whom they meet every day. I am deeply convinced that only she mediates the grace from the Lord for them so that they can be witnesses all the time. They have been growing in mental, spiritual and physical sense and have grown up into mature persons, now already fathers and mothers, except Vicka, who has remained wholly available to the pilgrims so far. She has not established a family, but has not joined any community either.

We are tempted at all levels to expect more from the visionaries than they can give or more than what they really are. Amazement and misunderstanding are possible here and, therefore, also condemnations. One thing is clear though: In fifteen years of Our Lady's school each of them has grown into a mature person and consciously remained a witness of faith, the way Our Lady also wants it.

— For children and even for adults it is often not easy to bear the burden of daily life, from regular school duties to family obligations, education, employment, etc. How have the children responded to the call of the Queen of Peace, how have they taken on and how are they been bearing, from a human point of view, this difficult obligation of transmitting and living Our Lady's messages?

When the visionaries get a message give it to the world. What they are saying is not their thought, nor has it anything to do with their way of life. And when they hear a message, they have to go on living and witnessing to others. We cannot compare their role with anyone else's, let alone then pass judgment on it. One thing is sure: They are the primary, persistent, and intrepid witnesses of Our Lady's presence. As far as I know, each of them is eager to respond to Our Lady's message in the best possible way. Likewise, they are constantly available and give witness to everyone who looks for them and desires to hear the message from their lips. Great is the grace, but, therefore, great also is the responsibility. I think I can say that they have responded well and that they are tireless in testifying to Our Lady's presence. Allowing for all that they had to go through from the beginning, with all the pressures from the then authorities, one must admit that they have been growing and developing quite "normally" on the personal level, and that they have successfully transmitted Our Lady's message. Moreover, it has reached the end of the world and is bearing its fruits. Our Lady is with them and she helps them carry the heavy burden of all obligations.

— Besides being a priest, you are also a psychologist. How do you find the visionaries in comparison with their age group, their fellow villagers? Can one say they are just ordinary children, or people, from Bijakovići, from Herzegovina, or does something nevertheless differentiate them?

I repeat that they are collectively and individually completely normal persons. They have fit into the life of the community and the Church, like many others. There is nothing special that would distinguish them from others, nor do they want to be different. They are aware that they have been chosen to be the bearers and propagators of Our Lady's messages, and tirelessly so.

I remember somebody having asked Vicka whether her life had changed because of the apparitions. She smiled and said, "Of course, you see, I've been preaching and speaking about the messages all the time, something that has been neither my wish nor my decision at all".

There is no other distinction except that they have been chosen, and that is by itself already a great distinction. However, this distinction is crucial in itself after all, for without the testimony of the visionaries and their perseverance Međugorje would not be what it is today: *The most powerful call to peace and the most persistent prophetic challenge in the modern world*. By that then they are also differentiated from others.

— One of the ways of spreading the messages of

the Queen of Peace from the parish of Međugorje are the prayer meetings of the visionaries with the faithful. There is no Continent and, one can freely say, no country in the world that the children have not been to. How do the faithful experience the visionaries?

Every pilgrim wants to meet at least one of the visionaries. The first answer they are looking for is to see whether they are normal persons, whether there is something special about their life. And it is exactly this special quality that people are expecting to find. And this special quality can be found indeed, for they talk about meeting Our Lady personally, about what she looks like, what and how she speaks, and what she expects from us. It is here that the desired beginning of the response to Our Lady's messages happens. Although many pilgrims picture themselves the visionaries as something special, yet they remain deeply moved by their normality, simplicity, readiness to give a testimony. At times some would leave disappointed, for they had expected the visionaries to be what they neither are nor can be. If somebody comes with a conviction that he would solve all the problems, find an answer to all his questions, then he is very likely to be disappointed. But the one who comes to hear Our Lady's message with a wish to do it, he will always be delighted. I know that many wondered how it is possible that the visionaries can marry after all the experiences they have had in the visions. Some became disappointed for they wanted all the visionaries to go to monastery. A few were delighted by their decision to establish a family, to have children, for this becomes a proof for them that the world has a future, that it pays to decide for life.

— Let us now pass over to the parish of Međugorje. Before 1981 this parish had been like all parishes in Herzegovina, with traditional way of life of its inhabitants; what has been happening to it during the last fifteen years?

Too much has been happening in the parish community of Međugorje in these 15 years that it could be described. Everyone living here has his experiences and his history during Our Lady's apparitions, and so does every visitor. It is impossible to speak about the events in the parish without speaking about individuals and groups, and again, since nobody fully knows the secrets of hearts, no answer can be given, actually. So we have to satisfy ourselves with a very superficial answer, and that is that changes in religious, social, psychological and economic sense *are* happening in the parish community of Međugorje.

THE PARISH HAS STRONGLY RESPONDED TO THE APPARITIONS

— The changes are radical indeed. Today Međugorje and the villages of this parish are in every respect unrecognisable as compared with the time before Our Lady's appearance. Still, how have these changes affected the parish, spiritually and religiously?

The parish community of Međugorje responded strongly at the beginning of the apparitions. Many started praying and fasting, they were even ready to suffer on that account either by running the risk of imprisonment or by having to keep watch day and night. At that time the response of the parish community was almost euphoric. In the course of time things have been subsiding, which is only normal. However, there is a danger now for the original experiences and the original intentions of Our Lady to be forgotten, for the first love and the original ardour to be lost. There is a real danger for the spiritual to be forgotten in the parish, and for the materialisation of relations with Our Lady and with each other to occur. The danger is real, but I am confident that we shall overcome it, for there are individuals and families who follow Our Lady's messages in their everyday life and work. One is no longer living at the beginning of the apparitions, which is understandable, but we have to endeavour not to forget Our Lady's original intention with us and with those coming here. The parish community must never forget that it was chosen and that Our Lady said that we were so important to her that without us she could not do what God had entrusted to her in these times.

— Studies and books should be written about sociological, psychological and demographic changes that Međugorje has undergone. If I am well informed, such dissertations and researches are already underway. In this question, let us limit ourselves to the acceptance of the messages in the parish of Međugorje and to how they are being

lived. Accordingly, how has the village participated in the living of the messages and the daily apparitions?

I have already partly answered that question. Without the original strong response of the parish community and every individual, the Communists would have succeeded in stopping God's deed. The perseverance of the visionaries and their families and of the whole parish community was of vital importance here. When the parish community was put under pressure (and one of the pressures was also having to stand guard at 11 points, and everybody knew it was unnecessary!), the then Communist authorities obviously wanted to stir up rebellion of the parish community against the visionaries and the events, so that they could then have a pretext to "intervene" according to their scenario: for they had to listen to the wishes of the people and protect them. The parish community shouldered a crushing burden. Our Lady would have it so. Everybody had to be involved in order to bear the pressure and move forward.

It is difficult, however, to say how individuals are living the messages. There is a nice number of faithful in the parish community that is living the messages, coming to mass and the prayers daily, taking part in the prayers on Apparition and Cross Mountains and in adoration of Jesus in the most holy Sacrament of the Altar. There are those, and that is a fact, who have lost every religious sense of the apparitions and value everything in terms of business and money. For such people, pilgrims are not those who seek God here, but those who one can take advantage of, who one can charge heavily, cheat, whose car one can steal. This must not surprise us either, for in a message of hers Our Lady said that where she and her Son come, Satan, the destroyer, also sneaks in. Nevertheless, let us not forget that without the participation of the parish community it would be hard to imagine the course of the apparitions and of their living.

As for everyday experience of Our Lady's apparitions today, I would like the hour of her appearance to be consecrated time at the level of the parish community. How nice it would be if every shop, every restaurant and every café stopped working and if everybody started praying the rosary at that holy hour of Our Lady's visitation. Everything would look different among us.

— When I think about the apparitions and the way of their spreading, and about the effect of the messages, I personally experience them in the form of concentric circles. First the children are illuminated by the messages, then their families and neighbours, then the parish and our whole nation, and finally the whole world. If I am right, will you please describe the dynamics of this propagation.

Exactly. The visionaries are the primary witnesses, then the parish community including everybody in the parish, from the smallest child to the parish priest and the Sister. Thanks to the suffering of the Franciscans, of the visionaries and of the whole parish community, the news of the apparitions spread fast and far. As early as in the first year people started coming from all parts of the world: they would see it for themselves, experience it, get convinced and when they returned home they would continue doing what Our Lady had told. Today one can literally say that the message has spread to the end of the world. It was the Italians who responded first, then the faithful from the German speaking areas. Then the English and French speaking areas opened. As for Europe, people come from all its parts and countries, and also from the whole world.

APPARITIONS HAVE BROUGHT ABOUT CHANGES IN THE WHOLE WORLD

— **Let us go back to the beginnings of Our Lady's apparitions. In 1981 Eastern Europe was still a world behind the iron curtain, and so was, of course, the former Yugoslavia. In such conditions of hard-core Communism and atheism occurrences started which fundamentally deny all Communist tenets. Can we, or would it be too exaggerated to, look for the beginning of the end of Communism in Međugorje?**

I think it is not exaggerated to talk about it. Tito died in May 1980. Many in the world wondered what would become of Yugoslavia. Many prophesied its death, but in any case a lot of problems. However, nobody could even anticipate the fall of Communism in the whole Europe, the fall of the Berlin wall, and free elections in Communist countries. Some ten years after the apparitions all that happened indeed. The fact is that this happened after the beginning of and during Our Lady's apparitions. Whoever chooses to do so, does not exaggerate if he discovers and accepts a deep connection between Our Lady's apparitions and the end of Communism, but whoever does not accept it, should not be blamed for that. For me it is very interesting when I recall that, during the first interrogation, the visionaries themselves were accused of fabricating the apparitions in order to destroy Communism. It happened, like in the Gospel, that the possessed had recognised Jesus before others did.

— We agree, then, that the beginning of the end of Communism in the world starts with the apparition of the Queen of Peace in the parish of Međugorje, that is with the acceptance of Our Lady's messages both by the visionaries and the parishioners and by the faithful from more distant places. Let us recall those first days; will you describe how it was all happening.

It is impossible to describe everything that was happening. Recalling the very beginnings, we know that the visionaries claimed that they had seen Our Lady on June 24, 1981 and that their testimony set the faithful multitude in motion, followed very soon by the Communist resistance, imprisonment of the parish priest, the curate and some civilians. However, now after 15 years, we can say that the little ones who came to believe and followed Our Lady have carried the day. The truth

Our Lady recites in her Magnificat with Elisabeth, comes about here, too. God exalts the lowly, takes the side of the oppressed and gives them right, but he brings down the haughty, the conceited, the mighty, with the might of his right arm.

Everything went at an incredible speed. Međugorje has caused no accident after all, although many caused accidents about Međugorje. In this anniversary many enemies have personally laid down their spears and arrows and accepted Međugorje, and the main enemy, the organiser of the resistance, exists no more as an establishment. It is gone.

— The visionaries were under terrible pressure from the authorities and the police, and so were the parishioners and the priests. Many of them were convicted, and the court proceedings and the sentence against the then parish priest Father Jozo Zovko are world famous. How did everybody suffer in those times, then?

Everybody suffered, but nobody slackened off. When on August 18 the church was closed, and Fr. Jozo Zovko taken to prison, the police searched the parish apartment and interrogated the sisters and other priests. Everything was blocked the whole day. The celebration of the evening Mass was to be prevented. The people were praying behind the barricade on the bridge. What a difference to all the barricades set up exactly 10 years later! The barricades opened up. The church filled up all at once. All the present testify it was very moving. One of the visionaries said, "Nothing is going to happen to Father Jozo". The whole church was crying. The pressures continued at all levels, psychical and physical ones. There started interrogations, search of false witnesses, imputation of written slogans, accusations of innocent people. Nobody will ever be able to express all that we had to go through, but one thing is always certain: many have become witnesses of faith. People suffered with joy, hope and love. I was told that a member of the special police from Sarajevo, for they had also been engaged, had said, "They have called us here as if it were a war, but everything is peaceful here like in a graveyard".

IT IS IMPORTANT TO ACCEPT THE MISSION

— **The next question I am going to ask you, has repeatedly been put both to you and to the visionaries, as well as to others. The question is: Why did Our Lady, the Queen of Peace appear just in Međugorje? Can this question be asked at all, and is there an answer to it?**

This question is frequently asked, and it is quite normal to ask why Our Lady chose Međugorje. I think after all that nobody can answer this question. I am personally convinced that she could as well have chosen any parish community, but I am equally convinced that any parish community that might have been chosen instead, would have one smaller and one bigger hill, and a church in-between, for these are simply indispensable spaces for Our Lady's school of peace, just like every school has to have its rooms for study and exercise. That is why it is no longer important why she has chosen Međugorje, what matters is to accept the mission and remain tireless in Our Lady's school. He who fails to understand this, may he be daily with the visionaries, in Međugorje or Bijakovići, will always be outside of what Međugorje, by Our Lady's wish, means.

— Now I would ask a few questions about the fruits of Međugorje. First, let us go back to the first question in this interview: What do you consider the most important fruits of the apparitions of the Queen of Peace?

The original aim of Our Lady's school is to educate us for peace. There is no peace yet, either in political or any other sense. Many individuals are still without peace of soul, and so are consequently the families, the Church and the whole world. Maybe we can say it could have been even worse; but we can also say it could have been better. For this reason I would suggest not to talk about the fruits just like that, for we cannot explain the conflicts in the parish community, in the diocese, in the nation, in the world. I certainly do not mean to say that there are no rich fruits. Namely, for me the greatest fruit is that many people have stirred spiritually, started praying and fasting, being converted, and accepted the way of peace and reconciliation. I know that many prayer groups have been set up, monastic communities are being created - all as a fruit of conversion responses. Everything is still in its infancy though. Such things take time. But a good seed and a good soil promise good fruits.

We must not forget that the parish community of Međugorje is changing both in economic and social respect, owing to the pilgrims. Such changes are inevitable, but they may assume dangerous forms and bear some bitter fruits. This does not, however, jeopardise what Our Lady intended originally. Only care should be taken.

— Fasting, penance, peace, prayer, conversion – these are the words most frequently associated with the apparitions in the parish of Međugorje. How much is the Church – both the living Church as a community of the faithful, and the official Church – affected by these changes?

The best answer to this question would be to take Our Lady's messages and quote her. On the one hand she is patient: she keeps speaking, goes on walking with us, gives thanks to all those who respond, keeps calling everybody to do something for their brothers who are far away, who do not convert. But we have to avoid painting everything black and white about Međugorje; we must not give an impression to those from outside or to the adversaries of Međugorje as if everything were good and perfect here, and nothing else. One thing is sure: Through Our Lady's messages many people in the Church have rediscovered prayer and fasting and decided for them. Let me tell you the experience of a pilgrim priest. He said to me: "I have realised here that in 30 years of preaching I have never talked to people about fasting, for example to explain to them why, how, when to fast, or what risks and advantages it brings. I would mention fasting sometimes, of course, at least during Lent. Now when I read the Bible, I wonder how it was possible for me to overlook this message when it appears on almost every page. Jesus used to fast, spoke about fasting, said that his people would also fast. How was it possible, I never cease wondering, and I am afraid that there are still many messages waiting for my conversion to be discovered by me." In his encyclical of March 25, 1995, the Pope called everybody to fast and pray, courageously and humbly. I cannot say there are no changes, but I wish I saw more of them, both in every individual and in the official Church.

— **The vivacity, the impact of Međugorje in the Catholic Church is omnipresent, it has affected all classes of the faithful. How much has Međugorje influenced the official Church?**

It is difficult to speak of an influence on the official Church. But it would be good if such an influence occurred, for Međugorje calls us to live the Gospel. A change should occur both in our preaching and in the practice. Many preachers are in danger of stooping to the socio-psychologico-pedagogical level, without going into the secret of God's presence in the Eucharist, nor are they able to initiate others into it. So changes and effects can be discussed only subject to encountering this secret. And such an encounter can occur only through prayer and fasting, which then manifest themselves in the concrete life with others.

— There is, it is quite clear, or am I wrong, a parallel course of influence on the faithful and on the official Church. I mean the numerous statements of the local bishop, and also of the commissions that have been officially examining the authenticity of the apparitions. Is their a convergence, a meeting point, of these two courses, how big is the probability of their converging into one course?

The more of the faithful revive their life with God and renew their life in the love for the neighbours, the more the official Church will be opening. This is happening at the level of parishes and dioceses. This can be seen in the fact that we from Međugorje are already being invited officially by the bishops of many dioceses, but there are also those who do not allow any of the visionaries or priests from Međugorje to come to their areas. With time Međugorje will be accepted. It will happen inaudibly, like spring. Hostilities and attacks are abating, many enemies have become friends, many uninterested ardent bearers of the message, some again have become tired. I think that everything is going as it could go with us in our situation. Let us remember, from the very beginning both the Church and civilian authorities were against Međugorje. With what impetuosity did they swoop down upon us to knock us down: imprisonment, external pressures, as well as the pressures from the Church authorities, more exactly by the bishop, bans, backbiting, slander. What matters is that the hostilities, which originated from various sources, are not growing but rather subsiding, and one day Međugorje shall "pass". And fasting and prayer will be the most important things then, too.

PEOPLE OF ALL CATEGORIES GO ON PILGRIMAGE TO MEĐUGORJE

— Who are the visitors to the parish of Međugorje? Can the social structure of the pilgrims be determined?

Međugorje is visited by all categories of people. All ages, the young and the old, the unlearned and the learned, the healthy and the sick, the faithful and the unfaithful, laymen and church dignitaries, politicians and soldiers. And again, not only the Catholics, but also other Christians, and members of other religions.

— I often wonder how people get to know of apparitions, for example in Mexico, in certain parts of USA, Australia? How do they find out about Međugorje?

The message spreads and is spreading by all the means of communication. Radio, television, newspapers, but the most important way is personal witnesses, those who had come here to see and then, after having returned home, started telling others and bringing others here. That is the most powerful and the most reliable way of spreading the message. The news read in the newspapers or seen on television is easily forgotten, but living witnesses cannot be overlooked. In this respect, many in the world are simply tireless. A lot of books have been written, many magazines are already coming out. The message is spreading.

Ant this is one of the wonders. One only should be able to see it. Sometimes somebody accuses us friars that we have made it all look as it is now, through our propaganda. We are really not that powerful. Nobody has ever given a single penny for propaganda, nor have there been any teams of managers to work on the "sale of the message". That is Our Lady' doing. It was not the friars, but Our Lady who was calling, and the friars, together with the visionaries, were only making effort to receive those coming here.

— Pilgrims come from the most remote corners of the world. What is it that motivates many to come to this, officially still unrecognised shrine?

The testimony of the people who have already been here most often motivates others to come. Change of life, then so many healings – both physical and spiritual ones – are a motivation enough for others to come. It is often lightly said that only those with some problems, the sick and the like, come here. Now many are coming, for in Međugorje they started praying and want to develop spiritually. They look for more information and formation, that is, for growth and development. It is here that we become even more responsible for them. But maybe we are in danger of jeopardising the formation of the people coming here by fast cars and loud music, night bars etc. It is a great responsibility, for if the one who has received information cannot pray here in the church, on Podbrdo or on Križevac peacefully, he will stop coming. In other words, people come in search of God, and Mary can help in that, and she does so.

70

— I am making this interview with you because you are constantly in Međugorje, among pilgrims, or at prayer meetings somewhere in the world. What is it that pilgrims expect on their way to this village, to this shrine of Our Lady?

I have already partly answered that: A pilgrim wants to meet witnesses who live the message, and to have time for prayer, an opportunity for confession, adoration, to experience peace. A sick person certainly expects to be healed, but everybody is looking for the experience of faith and of God's love.

And again we in the parish must take a good care and not think that people would keep coming if we have better houses or roads, although this is needed, of course, but they will be coming if we are for them a school of spirituality and a support on the way to God.

GOD GUIDES THE HISTORY OF EVERY INDIVIDUAL AND NATION

— Međugorje is the parish of the whole world, this is emphasised not only by the priests who live in it but also by the visiting priests and pilgrims. Its landmarks – recognisable in the whole world – are St James Church, Križevac and Podbrdo, the three landmarks which attract pilgrims. Will you please point out the most essential points about each of the three, what they mean to the faithful, what they mean in the religious life?

It is already known that Podbrdo, Križevac and the parish church are three places of prayer, three parts of this shrine of the Queen of Peace. Podbrdo is like Bethlehem, the beginning of everything, with Križevac the way of suffering continues, and in the church the faithful meet the resurrected Christ in the sacraments and in the Mass sacrifice. The outer way from Podbrdo via Križevac to the church indicates the inner process in the soul, a process which should occur to every man if he wants to attain to peace. That is why I said in an earlier answer that these spaces are indispensable for Our Lady's school. And besides, the hills in the biblical revelation are the places on which God reveals Himself. From Mt. Sinai and Horeb to Tabor and Calvary. Jesus liked hills and Our Lady liked them, too. We, too, should come to love them, for it is a preparation of the soul for the meeting with the living Christ in the sacraments. There is another symbolism. Namely, the man should leave the valley, fog, darkness, climb the hill, get rid of the everyday routine and open his soul to God.

— Earlier in some texts, the God's intention and plan for this parish was clearly expressed, pointed out. In everything. Some moves and projects cannot be qualified as coincidences: first, the church in Međugorje is one of the largest in Bosnia and Herzegovina, its construction started long ago, and as if there were a purpose in all that. Then the construction of the cross on Šipovac in 1933...

I believe that God guides the history of every individual, every community, every nation. Now that the apparitions have happened, and that it is happening what is happening, it is allowed to see and recognise God's plan in everything. One should recognise God's plan and cooperate with it. I am positive that every man, if he tries to do good and to love God, will discover God's plan in his life. Even in the very problems and difficulties he will recognise a section of the road which is fitted into his salvation.

It is important to be patient with God and perseveringly cooperate with Him.

— There are more coincidences that human intellect cannot circumvent, although they are hard to explain: namely, the parish is consecrated to St James, the patron of pilgrims, and Međugorje is the largest pilgrim centre in the world today. Was not the hand of God at work here again?

Yes. Now that Međugorje has become one of the meeting-places of pilgrims, it is again permitted to recognise the hand of God. It would be interesting to know what inspired those who consecrated this parish to St James, the patron of pilgrims. They certainly could have had no idea of what would be happening. You see, that is not important. They did what they should have done: establish a parish, put it under the patronage of one of God's favourites and preach the Gospel.

— One of the everyday messages of the Queen of Peace is the call to peace. However, with the breakdown of Communism our homeland Croatia and Bosnia and Herzegovina have gone through the greatest sufferings in the second half of the twentieth century. Will you compare this peace of Our Lady and the war destruction.

On the third day of apparitions, June 26, 1981 Our Lady gave the message of peace: *Peace, peace, peace, only peace. Peace between God and men and peace among men.*

It was also made clear: Pray and fast, through prayer and fasting you can even ward off wars and natural disasters. On June 26, 1991, towards evening, ten years later sharp, the first bombs were dropped on the Ljubljana airport. In 1981 none of us could have even thought of war in the classical sense in our country, nobody even dared to dream of the downfall of Communism. And when the war started, many were still saying there would be no war. It is clear now how short-sighted we were. It would be better if we did not have to admit it but it is so. Besides, it is also clear how weak of faith we are. When God speaks, His word has to be taken seriously. Even if we could not anticipate the war, we could at least have started and continued praying and fasting. By the time we realise that a war is possible, it seems to be already too late. The waves of war seem to have subsided, but Our Lady has not withdrawn her message: Let us pray and fast, let us convert, for many evils are threatening. They ought to be averted.

However, the world often behaves like an addict, like an alcoholic or junkie. When you talk to one, everything seems to be clear to him, he is aware of the dangers and what is going to happen if he does not stop, but then he goes on in the same manner up to the point of self-destruction, or, if he is lucky, of cure. I reiterate: Our Lady has not stopped coming or speaking; do not let us sleep, do not let God's call through Our Lady go past us.

— The parish of Međugorje has been spared war destruction, all time during the war it has been a centre of peace, and many initiatives for aiding the afflicted have been coming through Međugorje. Will you say what Međugorje meant for the Croatian people who were afflicted, and what for those who felt the call and wanted to help the afflicted?

Crowds of people have been passing through the Međugorje shrine, through Our Lady's school. The first two and most important lessons in Our Lady' school are: *To decide for God*, and then, like Mary who visited Elisabeth, *to decide for the neighbour*. Many said their *yes* to God here, and then, like Mary, learned of our sufferings and came to visit and help us.

— The importance of Međugorje should not be circumvented, either in our people or in the world. You have witnessed and participated in all the events before the war, during the war and now in the post-war time. What in your opinion has this parish meant for the Croatian people, for the Croatian state, and what for the world viewed from the heavy and painstaking struggle for the recognition of Croatia and for the recognition of the right for the Croatian people to independence?

Inspired by Our Lady's message many have come, got familiar with us, taken a liking to us and took our side when the aggressor went with his fist and boot against us. The help of pilgrims is great, not only in material, but also in moral and political sense. If anybody understood what this war was about, then it was the pilgrims, who brought their connections and influence to bear on their politicians trying to help us in this way as well. I think we are not aware of the amount of the help that came through the Međugorje pilgrims. Let us at least be thankful.

— **In the concatenation of unfortunate circumstances many, even our neighbours in Europe, did not know of Croatia and the Croatian people. They came to know us only through Međugorje. Is it presumptuous to assert that Croatia and Bosnia and Herzegovina have become clearer to the world thanks to the Međugorje apparitions?**

It may be said for a great part of pilgrims that they learned of us Croatians and Catholics through their visits to Međugorje. We have to be realistic, though: Who dared to speak to the pilgrims about the Croats and Croatian suffering, for example, while they were coming here during Communism? One could have done much more, but the question is whether one dared to. Who were the guides of those pilgrims, what were they saying to them, what did those young people know about themselves and about us, if they were Croatian at all, and they were not all Catholics, or Croats?!

Much more could have been done, but we are thankful for this much, too!

— **Speaking about these "socio-political" questions, which cannot be skipped, one should also** say something about the humanitarian dimension of Međugorje during the 1991-1996 period. Namely, during this period a lot of humanitarian organisations were operating through Međugorje. Can one describe or estimate the humanitarian aid that reached the afflicted and had been initiated by the love for this village?

Some facts could be given, but it would be all incomplete. Many used to stint themselves in order to give to us. From the first war days until now.

— Who were the people engaged in these humanitarian activities? What is their nationality, their financial status, education, age?

These humanitarians come from richer countries, which is quite understandable. Italians, Austrians, Germans, French, Belgians, Dutch, English, Irish and Americans. They are of all ages and of both sexes, but always the richest in material things. As for their profession, I used to meet people from all walks of life: from common workers to doctors, psychologists, professors...

— Is it only the faithful or are there unbelievers among them? If there are unbelievers, what is their motive?

I would not know, the people who were coming motivated by the love for the Croatian people were pilgrims, and *ipso facto* mostly believers.

— Apart from the humanitarian aid, there were also some other actions that helped to inform the world about our sufferings. How was this realised?

In the same way as the news of Our Lady's apparitions was spreading. All kinds of mass media, that used to convey the news and messages before the war, kept informing the faithful of the sufferings, and calling for help.

— **One of the results of Međugorje are prayer groups inspired by Our Lady's apparitions. How were these groups coming into being, in which countries are they present, how many are they, and how large is their membership?**

It is Our Lady's wish that we pray individually, in the families and that prayer groups be formed. Such groups came into being because the pilgrims who had come, heard and accepted the message, invited their friends and started praying together. These groups can be found in all places from which people have been on pilgrimage to Međugorje.

Nobody knows for certain how many prayer groups, inspired by the call from Međugorje, there are, but I think it is not exaggerated to speak about thousands of smaller and larger groups.

— **How do prayer groups act and what is their purpose?**

The purpose of prayer groups is to help individuals to keep a spirit of prayer and to grow properly, for a group lives on individuals, while individuals get help and control from the group. It is best if a priest leads a prayer group, or at least takes part from time to time.

— **The influence of prayer groups on their environment is probably considerable; have you got the elements to describe that with?**

Some prayer groups remain only at the level of a prayer meeting, which again may last differently. The ideal time would be up to two hours of prayer, song, conversation, Scripture reading. Whichever group is growing in Our Lady's spirit, becomes active on the social plan, too. The aid that the Croatian people had received, mainly came through prayer groups, which engaged themselves, collected funds and took an active part in bringing and distributing the aid.

Prayer groups all over the world breed spiritual vocations, cherish true prayer spirit. I know the groups that take care of captives, the sick, children – depending on the needs of the people in their place.

— **Are priests, or bishops involved in the activity of prayer groups?**

Priests are getting more and more involved, a bishop here and there, but there is nothing spectacular at this level. And indeed, it is not good if a group remains without a priest. In such cases groups have to be patient and remain in simple prayer and be available in various activities, until they are accepted. A parish priest told me once that he had been against Međugorje at first and everything related to it, including, of course the prayer group. But when he heard that the prayer group was praying for him as a priest, rather than for his accepting the apparitions, he accepted both the group and Međugorje, for, as he said, it was Our Lady's spirit to pray for priests, and not to criticise them.

— What is the co-operation of the parish person-nel, the priests from Međugorje and prayer groups like?

I think it is not possible to talk about special co-operation. When prayer groups come to Međugorje or organise pilgrimages, we do our best here for them: lectures, prayer meetings, etc. Prayer groups often arrange conferences, and meetings in general, and invite some of us priests and visionaries. Here we also do what we can, but we cannot do much, for there are more and more invitations just from prayer groups.

SPIRITUAL FRUITS

— Fruits are something you recognise a thing by. In its fifteen-year-old history Međugorje has also had rich fruits. Will you specify all that has been inspired by Međugorje and all that has come to be – in these fifteen years – thanks to the appari-tions of the Queen of Peace.

One should start from ourselves. The Međugor-je evening programme, which is a special mark of the Međugorje message consisting of the prepara-tions for the Mass, the celebration of the Mass and prayers after the Mass, as well as of Eucharist Ado-ration, prayer in front of the cross, outings to Pod-brdo and Križevac – are first spiritual fruits. They have spread all over the world. It is a kind of a land-mark at the spiritual level.

A lot of peace centres, prayer groups, radio sta-tions, newspapers, magazines have come into be-ing. A special mention should be made of two com-

munities: "The Oasis of Peace"and "Fully Yours –
Through Mary to Jesus", which came to be as a direct response to Our Lady's messages.

— I reiterate that your meetings with pilgrims are daily and numerous. You know the soul of pilgrims. What changes, most recognisable ones, have occurred in people?

The most recognisable changes occurred at prayer level. A lot of people have started praying. That is where everything starts. Where the response to prayer fails, nothing further can happen. Many have become aware that fasting is at least necessary. These are two basic and fundamental answers. I could not believe that people prayed so little until I started meeting Our Lady's calls on the one hand and the people who understand it is necessary to pray on the other. When one starts praying and fasting, other things may start happening, too.

— What is most essential for a believer to realise the beneficial change?

A change can only occur subject to the acceptance of a walk with Mary, the Queen of Peace. What we have here is a school. You can master something if you learn. Prayer, as a meeting with God, is a condition for a beneficial change.

— Fasting, penance, peace, conversion: Will you please describe the situation before Our Lady's appearance and now. What has been achieved? Do people fast, convert, is peace coming?

Something is happening, but certainly not as

81

much as it should. It is clear that a lot of people from the parish community had responded at first and then stopped short engaging in other matters. Too few are taking part in the evening programmes now, at adorations also very few, a bit more on Podbrdo, and on Križevac fewer again. The attendance of the young people from the parish community is especially low. The spiritual fruits in the parish are now difficult to recognise. The material situation is different. Here the changes are obvious. A lot of cafés, restaurants have been opened. It is there that many spend their evenings and nights instead of joining in the evening programme. It seems to me that there is less peace in the hearts of the young here now. The problem is that many have stopped and are not journeying with Our Lady any more.

— You have written a book on Our Lady's messages in Međugorje. What are the key messages, will you repeat them?

The key messages are: Peace, as a goal for everybody, through conversion in prayer and fasting, and in faith and love. Practically, Our Lady wants us to pray the whole rosary daily, to go to confession monthly, to read the Bible, and to go to Mass as often as possible.

— The Queen of Peace, the messages of the Queen of Peace, have influenced many to change their way of life. Which are the most pronounced changes, how deeply do they affect human soul?

Many have changed, for example, they started praying, a bit fasting, many have stopped blaspheming, etc., but signs of fatigue are beginning to show. So Međugorje attracts our people from the parish and its surroundings only for major feasts. For many there is no more any stronger incentive. Everything is ordinary for them. I cannot understand that the time of Our Lady's apparition has not entered the consciousness of our people as something special, extraordinary, wonderful. And we should not possibly forget this. There are individual persons who go on, but to my personal regret I must admit they are too few. Much more response is shown by the people from outside.

However, it can be said that people fast and pray, that those coming as pilgrims presently convert more.

— Conversion is an unavoidable topic of Međugorje. From the conversion of lukewarm believers, to the conversion of unbelievers, or the conversion of those who used to be believers once and then a good part of their life unbelievers or even opponents of faith. Will you describe the stages of conversion and what caused people most to convert?

We have to be careful when talking about conversion. It is a process for a whole lifetime. The first stage of conversion for us baptised is always a call to renounce evil, and then to go on growing in good. In our case it is especially a call to give up and overcome unrest and all that causes unrest and to open more and more to peace which is, Our Lady has repeated it so many times, a gift of God. But our co-operation is indispensable, too.

In meeting the visionaries and the persons who received the favour of being healed, many started their coming out of darkness and sin, and returning to God. There were visible signs in the sky and on the sun, claim many, which prompted them to change their lives. However, we have to be aware that these incentives have to continue being lived in everyday life.

— One of the fruits of Međugorje is prayer. Here people simply learn how to pray, or meet prayer for the first time. How has Međugorje influenced the acceptance of prayer, how does it act on pilgrims after their return home?

This is the greatest favour God gives here through Mary: Many have started to pray and got a desire for prayer. What happens when they return home is difficult to say. Those that join prayer groups have a chance of remaining on the way of prayer, and those who remain alone, I am afraid, might have coming to them what happened to many in the parish: from ardent devotees at the beginning of apparitions, they have returned to Sunday Mass obligation and remained there. It will be very difficult to restart them.

God leaves us free. He does not want our spiritual life to depend on everyday extraordinary miracles. And with many, the prayer life fits hardly into the everyday routine. In the parish community, likewise, whoever comes to the evening programme or takes part in the prayer group, is on the way with Mary.

— What would you say about the importance of

84

prayer in everyday life, not only to those coming here as pilgrims but to people in general, especially at this time of fast living, television, manipulation with people?

As food and drink are a condition for our physical life, so is prayer for spiritual life. Many are spiritually dead. The grace that God offers us through Mary may be compared with spiritual awakening. He who wakes up, if he does not get up immediately, is very likely to fall asleep again. A special intervention was needed for our awakening; in order to remain awake, we have to cooperate. Just like in ordinary life: if one is driving at high speed, he needs more time and strong brakes to come to a halt. Today's man is in great danger of dying spiritually. Prayer, as a meeting with God, must set us free from slavery to material things. It seems to me that Gods lets us, like parents do with mischievous children, fly, get tired, maybe get bruised all over, in order to come to a stop. We'd better do so in time. God is trying through Mary. All those who have come to a stop and obeyed know what it means. Only let us not forget that.

— How to learn how to pray? Is there a recipe for that?

Once they asked Mother Theresa from Calcutta, "How to pray better?" She smiled and said, "Pray more". This is the only recipe, there is no other. Many, unfortunately, find a recipe for prayer only when they meet with difficulties. Our Lady urges us not to seek God because of our needs, but out of love of God.

THE IMPORTANCE OF INNER HEALING

— In the parish of Međugorje, through the intercession of the Queen of Peace, physical and spiritual healings occur. Both were reported in the press and dealt with in various books. For this occasion, and the fifteenth anniversary *is* a great occasion, will you point out what is the most essential for both kinds of healings.

Neither Lourdes and Fatima, nor Međugorje or any other shrine have been given by God to replace hospitals and medical services, although healings are happening at all levels. When miraculous healings do happen, then it is first and foremost because of the testimony of faith. Such people become witnesses. That is what is happening here at Our Lady's intercession. Just like in the Gospel, Jesus is working wonders to show his divine mission, that people may come to believe. It is true that everywhere in churches and prayer groups many miraculous healings would occur if there were more prayer inspired by faith and love.

— Are there disappointments when it comes to healings? Namely, people come with hope, and have to return without changes. In fact, are there those who return disappointed?

It is difficult to know in what frame of mind one returns. Disappointments are possible, and they have probably occurred. Every moment of suffering is hard, and one looks for an easement. However, whenever we pray, one should say, "Your will be done!" Our Lady teaches us to pray so as to be able to carry our crosses like Jesus did His. This seems to me to be a condition for special healings, too.

In order to keep ourselves from disappointments, we have to understand properly both the prayer and the shrine, and the role of prayer and of faith in general. A lot of the sick come without asking for healing, for they have accepted their crosses, they come to pray. I know many persons who have accepted their cross, their suffering, and this is most important for healing. We all know that there are people who are healthy and young, who have everything, but still they are spiritually dissatisfied and restless. The inner healing is what matters most; that is to say, we should endeavour that our love heals, our hope, mutual respect, our inner freedom, peace, and all the rest will take a turn for the better.

— When speaking of hope and disappointment, my thoughts take me to our times. Namely, the technical and technological civilisation, in which we live, leaves us simply no time for thinking. You are known as a man who meditates a lot. How to become absorbed into oneself, to meditate, nowadays at all?

The most important thing is to take time for prayer, and in order to do that, we have to be free, not to slave, and again, for us to be able to get rid of slaving to television, games etc., we have to receive grace. Do not ask what comes first, but start praying. Here we have extraordinary, better to say, all the conditions for prayer: the church, the chapel, adorations, Podbrdo, Križevac, evening adorations. That is how Our Lady teaches us. I have been organising weeks of fasting and prayer for quite a long time now. What is offered here is an important experience of spiritual life.

— **In what way do the young participate in Me-đugorje? Is there any specific work with them, or are they in the crowd with others?**

As concerns the young from the Croatian people in general, they come from those parishes and prayer communities where they have been organised. I think they are too few, though. For special feasts the young give us a "surprise" by coming here on foot, but I have not heard of their being converted, for to convert would mean for them leaving cafés and discos empty, reducing the number of drug addicts. Unfortunately, this is rather growing, taking disastrous proportions.

— **Our young people are threatened by many dangers – first of all drugs. How to save them from all these evils?**

I think that it is easy to save the young from all evils, including drugs, under one condition: that the adults, elders, get converted. The young are the victims of those who are ready to destroy all our youth in order to make money. I do not understand how this is possible. They are war profiteers. I wonder why nobody can put a stop to these dealers. If we loved our life, our young, more, we could defend them. Everybody has failed here: the politics, the police, the army, the Church. We are not fighting enough. People resign easily. Many think:

What do I care, it is not my child. Unfortunately, it will be yours and mine, ours and yours, bet your life!

— The young often object their not being taken care of, not being given a chance. How, in what way, should they be participants in the world, change it for the better?

We elders should teach the young to accept the world, to change it. But instead of healthy food we often give them poisoned one. Still, there are young people who, thank God, struggle, learn, study, complete their studies, come back as experts; they are going to act and change the world for the better. There are, on the other hand, young people who are in danger of thinking that everything should be turning around them. When I hear one of them say to me that his parents do not love him, I ask him immediately whether he loves his parents. Here they often pause to think.

—Are you satisfied with the number of young pilgrims from the world? What do these young people expect from the Queen of Peace and what do they find in this parish?

There could be more of them. Here I am stung to the quick again. I know of some organisers of pilgrimages who do not dare any more to bring the young, for in Međugorje night life continues when, according to all laws and regulations, it dies out in the nearby small towns. They can't keep their young at the evening prayer, because there are pastimes, from cafes to video-games, and I do not know what else. Those in the parish that own such premises should realise that they are digging a pit into which we are all going to fall.

If we fail to save Međugorje from such elements, the true pilgrim will stop coming, for he will be choked. He does not come to watch attractive neon signs, but to pray, eat and drink decently, and be quiet. Can you understand what it means when a crowd of pilgrims are having an evening adoration outside, and the music is blaring from the nearby restaurant? Maybe they are right in expecting us all, especially the young, to give an example.

— **What experiences do they take home?**

Those that come and are well organised, leave with positive experiences. This is the reason that the big international prayer meeting of the young in early August lives on. At this time we organise everything for the young. I have been in this organisation from the beginning, but it is becoming more and more difficult, because our young people are slow in joining in; the young from our families do not come to these programmes, they go rather to their evening pastimes, and consequently the young pilgrim does not get enough incentive. I am speaking from my experience! The most difficult question asked by a pilgrim was: Am I going to hurt the feelings of the family I am staying with if I do not take any of the offered meat on Wednesdays?

OUR LADY HAS OPENED A SCHOOL OF PEACE IN MEĐUGORJE

At the beginning of the apparitions there were

90

comparisons between the apparitions of the Queen of Peace in Međugorje and other apparitions in the world. What makes them different and what alike?

It is the same Madonna with the same mission: to help us find Jesus. The difference is that Međugorje is only in the making, that everything is still in progress. Let me answer with the answer of a pilgrim. He said to me: "They asked me why I was going to Međugorje, Our Lady is here, too! I said: 'If my favourite singer, whose all cassettes and records I have, comes to sing live, I shall leave radio and TV and the cassette recorder and go to hear him. Our Lady is there live, that is why I am going.'" This is the difference at the moment!

— **The Queen of Peace has been in Međugorje for fifteen years, every day. When you come to think of previous apparitions (Fatima, Lourdes...), where the apparitions lasted short, what can you say, of course, as far as your priestly experience allows you, as to why this apparition has been lasting for so long?**

Anybody could try to answer this question. Every answer will have its share of truth. However, only Our Lady can fully answer this question, or somebody after everything has happened what is to happen. At present, none of us knows that. I think that Our Lady has been appearing for so long and on a daily basis, because she has opened a school of peace. And to be able to live in peace means first of all to be able to love, to forgive, to be merciful. It is a very difficult school, that is why it is lasting longer than usual. This answer could be added the fact that at the moment the world is more needy of peace than ever before. There are more and more of restless people. God is our peace, Mary is with us, so we can have peace.

— **Pilgrims, a lot of them, have been on pilgrimage to other shrines of Our Lady and to Međugorje. What are their experiences? Are different apparitions associated with their fruits?**

I remember a priest who assured me that every year he had been organising pilgrimages to different shrines. Each time he could say at the end it had been good. At the end of the pilgrimage to Međugorje, apart from the fact that it had been good, everybody wondered before parting: And what now?!? Something has to be done. For me as parish priest, this is the big difference between Međugorje and other places of pilgrimage: Međugorje activates – and that is important!

— **The Queen of Peace has inspired the establishment of many organisations, prayer groups, movements. In the parish itself various organisations and movements are active, from prayer ones to medical, humanitarian, ones. Father Slavko, will you please describe by name every organisation and movement, their importance and achievements, the purpose of their activity.**

I have already mentioned those two that are present here and were born with the apparitions. They are "The Oasis of Peace" and the Community "Queen of Peace, Fully Yours – Through Mary to Jesus". These two communities endeavour to live

92

Our Lady's message fully. Sister Elvira opened the house "Campo della vita" for the young with the drug problem. Međugorje attracted her. The experience is very useful. A community of French origin "Beatitudes" is also active here. Its mission is to bring pilgrim groups here and to help them in their spiritual growth. Other groups and humanitarian organisations have no direct relation to Međugorje as a place of prayer. By a combination of war circumstances the houses for pilgrims remained empty, but Međugorje was peaceful after all, so that many world organisations found accommodation just here in Međugorje, and so did UNPROFOR and now IFOR.

The importance of these organisations can be great on the social plan under war circumstances, but as for Međugorje, I do not think they have brought anything positive. On the contrary, it is well known that many "humanitarians" are either spies or lost and sick persons. Many are known to have brought and dealt drugs here. How much have they boosted the morale of the parish community by all that, nobody can answer. For the message of peace, in the Međugorje sense, these "humanitarians" have not done much, if they have not stopped this process in many places.

— We can see – by their numbers, by the way of their activity and by their effect – that these organisations and movements are significant. What do you expect the future of their work will be, what are they going to mean to the parish of Međugorje itself, as well as to numerous pilgrims?

93

I have been convinced from the beginning that the Međugorje spirit of Our Lady, in the spiritual sense, will live only in these prayer groups and communities. The parish is mainly going to turn, at best, into Martha who entertains Jesus all right, and devotes herself less to listening to the word.

We must not lose balance here on any account, and the greatest danger lies just here, that is, if materialism gets the better of us and kills our spirit, then what Our Lady wished is not going to happen. Her only wish is that our life be really in God and through God. And all the rest will then go its right course.

—— What is common to those many, mutually unknown persons that makes them work together for the benefit of people?

Those coming as pilgrims are certainly inspired by Our Lady's love for all of us and by a great urge to help others in whom they recognise Jesus Christ. That is actually the only motive of love of Jesus. All these people are united by Our Lady's love for the needy. She is a Mother. Many others from humanitarian organisations come because it is their job. Unfortunately, many have brought drugs and other vices along.

With the end of the war we hope that the need after all these humanitarian organisations will be reduced and that they will withdraw. Communities will remain and they will carry the spirit of prayer and serve the pilgrims.

— Now allow me a personal question to you: Make an essay about yourself, Father Slavko Bar-

barić, both as man and priest, fifteen years ago and now. To put it more freely: Have you personally undergone changes, or rather who used to be Father Slavko Barbarić before and who is he now?

In January 1982 I came to Međugorje from my studies in Germany. Since then I have been active here, with shorter or longer breaks. When I finished my studies, I had quite different plans and so did probably my community when they sent me to the university. Today I am a priest in a Marian shrine, which is in the making, and with my brethren and community I try to find for myself first an answer to Our Lady's messages and to help others to understand and live them. This especially affects the prayer life in the church and on the hills. Maybe I cannot speak so much of changes, but rather of a growth especially in prayer life, which is certainly very important.

— The result of your activity in the shrine of the Queen of Peace are numerous books, some of which have gone into fantastically large printing runs, as for example the book *Pray with the Heart*, printed in many languages. Are there enough books about Our Lady's apparitions, have they been written seriously and do they reflect the true picture of the Shrine?

I am not a writer by nature, nor has it ever been my dream. Working with pilgrims and following the dynamics of Our Lady's messages, I was trying to discover Our Lady's spirituality and to convey it in simple words. The titles of my books reflect what I understood as a journey with Our Lady towards peace: One starts with prayer, goes through reconciliation, Eucharist sacrifice, daily exercise in love and immersion into the secret of Eucharistic presence. For this reason the books have the following titles: *Pray with the Heart, Give Me Your Wounded Heart, Celebrate Mass with the Heart, In the School of Love, and Adore My Son with the Heart.*

There are many books about Međugorje in the world. Many are in fact experiences of pilgrims, conversions, healings, then a number of scientific essays, and finally what René Laurentin does: namely after a fundamental book he went on publishing an annual chronicle of events.

— This interview is slowly coming to its close. We have talked little about Međugorje today, when we are in the year of the fifteenth anniversary of the apparitions. What can Međugorje do by way of healing the wounds of our people after the war calamities?

Whoever comes and does what Our Lady is telling, he will be healed, first in his soul. Confession is a moment of meeting the forgiving and healing Jesus. Many have experienced the healing of their wounds just here. Međugorje is still, and it should remain such by all means, a powerful call to confession, reconciliation.

— You visit various countries in prayer meetings. What do people in these countries expect from the Queen of Peace and from Međugorje?

When you go at the invitations of people from other countries, then people simply want information, but even more prayer. By praying with us, prayers that we organise before and after Mass here, and by participating in Mass celebrations people grasp best what Our Lady asks of us and what it means for us when we respond.

— The following question is similar to an earlier one, but this time it is not about your personal life, but about the Catholic Church: What was the Church like at the beginning of the apparitions and what is it like today? Can we say that Međugorje has had a positive effect on the changes, and if yes, will you describe these changes.

I am afraid I must admit that I cannot see much change in the hierarchical stratum of the Church. The fact is that priests are coming in ever increasing numbers, bishops also, and even cardinals have started coming. These are certain changes, openings, after all. Many have stopped at the question *sanctioned* or *non-sanctioned*. This is an important question, but there should be no problems at all, for everything that is being asked for and done in Međugorje is recognised: to pray, to fast, to convert, to go to confession, to read Scriptures, to pray the rosary. This should have been and should be done regardless of the apparitions. And if the apparitions have helped one, this should not be questioned. One has remained on the pharisian level: not what Jesus does, but who has given him the authority to do so, and he put a stress on deeds. Maybe it is best to say: easy, patiently! We have to show fruits, and then first eyes and then doors will start opening, again easy and patiently. If Our Lady had been in a hurry to be recognised it would have happened long ago. She knows that what she demands is recognised.

The changes are already visible where people have started praying personally, in families and in prayer groups.

—Apart from all that has been said about the fruits of Međugorje, in this shrine many have experienced true conversion, have gone to confession and taken Communion after long years. Is a record being kept on the number of the confessed and Communion receivers? If yes, how would they compare with other shrines?

It is hard to say how many people have confessed, while the number of Communions could be ascertained to an extent. However, we still cannot compare with great and famous shrines of Our Lady such as Lourdes, Fatima, Guadeloupe, Chenstohowa etc. And as for confessions, this is something that confessors and the confessed know best. Confessions are heard daily in several languages. For major feasts up to a hundred priests would be hearing confessions for hours.

— A large number of pilgrims from almost all countries take part in the daily evening Mass and in the whole prayer programme. The Mass and other programmes, except for some short parts, are in the Croatian language. What is it that attracts these people daily to participate, although practically they do not understand a word?

A Mass is not understood by intellect. It is lived with the heart, and this takes time. Why do many of our people not change by coming to Mass? The answer is clear: They just rush in at the last moment and rush out first after the final blessing. Many do not even stay for seven Our Fathers, which we consider a votive prayer.

Our Lady asks of us to prepare for Mass. We do it an hour before by praying the rosary. We continue with the prayers after Mass, that is we remain with Jesus. The pilgrims, although they do not understand the language, take time to immerse into the secret of the Eucharist and feel well. This is the everyday Eucharistic miracle.

— The principal messages of Our Lady, from the first day of apparitions, are: peace, faith, conversion, prayer, fasting. We know that war is constantly present, the statistical data about faith practising are discouraging. In the torn conditions of everyday life there is no time for conversion, prayer, while fasting was almost forgotten. What I mean is that these principal messages of Our Lady directly cut into our conformist life and our conformist times. How to respond to the messages, how to live them?

One should make a decision. It is a great grace of Međugorje that people have started responding more readily. In replying to this question I would like to point out again: One should persevere, and this is not easy because the way of life, the stuff offered on television, radio, in the newspapers are often such as to kill the spirit and soul of a man, of a family, of the world. It seems to me that many understand and return only after they have hit their head against a wall. The response to these messages of fasting and prayer cannot any longer be understood as a pious exercise with a meaning at personal level. It seems to me that the Hamletish question could be modified to read: To fast and pray, and to be – or not to be. The culture of death is unfortunately appealing, bewitching and charming. Disappointment becomes necessary for many to discover lies and vanities of this world and to take a new course. These processes, however, are always related to bitterness and inner anger and nervousness, but end well. Peace is possible only in the freedom of heart. Peace will have to come.

— The war in Croatia and Bosnia and Herzegovina has caused pilgrims almost to stop coming to Međugorje. Nevertheless, all these five past years the most courageous have kept coming. In what way did Our Lady's messages live in those in the world who had already been on pilgrimage to Međugorje, and in those who wanted to come but could not because of the war?

As already said, whoever has joined a prayer group, whoever has introduced prayer into his family and remained faithful, his family has certainly become a family of peace. I know of many prayer groups in the world who truly live Our Lady's messages and bear rich fruits. During the war many were prevented from coming, but they were renewing prayer, organising prayer meetings for peace in our homeland, many of whom consider it their own and which many have fallen in love with through Our Lady. The war victims have urged many pilgrims to charity. They have become tireless in collecting and bringing aid. This is how the first and second mysteries of the joyful rosary have occurred. It was here that they said together with us, like Mary did: Here is the maid of the Lord! And then they heard of our calamity and hastened to our assistance, like Mary did. The prayer Our Lady is calling us to, coupled with fasting, breeds love for God and others. May it be so!

—And for the end, an unavoidable question: How do you see Međugorje in the future? Do you see its growth, or new fruits, and what effect is it going to have in the history of salvation?

Međugorje will be growing in the measure in which the visionaries, we in the parish and pilgrims will be growing. We are all responsible. What use would there be of Međugorje growing if we are not growing, and it has been given for our sake, for the sake of our spiritual growth and of our life with God.

The importance of Međugorje should not be shifted onto external levels, nor should it be viewed triumphantly. It is first and foremost an inner dimension. Personally I am not so much interested in what will be happening in the world. I am more interested in the parish community. If we compare everything with a river having its spring in Međugorje, then our responsibility is to keep the spring clean. If we manage that, then people will keep coming to drink. If we pollute this spring, nobody will be able to clean it downstream.

I do hope that God will give many souls in the

parish a spirit of prayer and fasting, of faith and love, so that there will always be powerful filters to keep the spring clean, and the parish and pilgrims will be like a tree planted by the running waters, bearing fruit at all times.

FIFTEEN YEARS OF MEĐUGORJE APPARITIONS

On June 24, 1981, on St John's feast, six children from Bijakovići, in the parish of Međugorje, while taking a stroll outside the village, saw a wonderful young woman with a baby in her arms in the region called Podbrdo (on the Hill of Crnica). On that day – when they, scared by the vision of the unusual figure, ran home and told their relatives and fellow villagers what had happened to them – a phenomenon began which has been provoking controversial reactions, but which day after day has been attracting the faithful from the whole world: the apparition of Our Lady, the longest in the history of Our Lady's apparitions in the world.

What was Bijakovići or Međugorje like fifteen years ago? Villages like other villages in the western Herzegovina. From time immemorial the people, cultivating their fields, growing tobacco and producing grapes and wine, have struggled to provide bread for their large families, to avert the everyday threat of poverty. Tobacco from these regions is well-known. It used to be smuggled into Bosnia and Croatia, because by selling it to tobacco stations one could at times not even get enough to buy an orange or an apple for the children let alone provide sustenance for the whole coming year. The history of tobacco, its price and the position of tobacco growers in Herzegovina make a segment of the political history of these people accustomed to wrong valuations and persecutions. The persecution of tobacco growers carried out by revenue officers and gendarmes between the two World Wars, and Milicija after World War II, is still in living memory of many, especially of the families whose one or several members were killed or wounded in those persecutions. Many a Herzegovinian, including those from Međugorje, had to spend some time in prison on charges of tobacco smuggling. Father Didak Buntić, a great Herzegovinian and Croatian Franciscan, on many occasions the protector of these people and their educator, in the early '20s of this century lodged a protest against the seizure of a kilo or so of tobacco that the novices used to bring along. The period after World War II did not bring any good for tobacco growers either. Tobacco cutters, for fear of being discovered by the police, used to work deep down in cellars and in hidden places, for if caught they would lose both tobacco and the cutting device and go to serve time in the infamous Ćelovina prison in Mostar.

Žilavka and Blatina, famous wines of this region, produced in the Middle Ages, too, served more to brace up the labourer's soul than for commercial sale, first of all because of the small estates that do not allow a larger production. Well, if one could not live here, the world was wide for him. Before the World War I only individual persons would go out into the world, while between the wars people started leaving their homes in large numbers and go mainly to South or North America. The first mass emigration started after World War II, when many fled across the border. In the early '60s a stream of people set out to "the temporary work" in Germany, Sweden, Switzerland, and many followed their star as far as the USA, Canada, Australia, South Africa and New Zealand. The irony of the political system would have it that many were declared "enemies" and objectionable, not only they but their relatives in the homeland, too.

It was in such an environment, both social and economic one, in a region always self-conscious religiously and nationally but never fanatical, that on a warm June evening in 1981, the events started, which first provoked disbelief of many but curiosity none the less, as well as the reactions of the authorities which spared none of the participants, from the visionaries, their relatives and priests to the visitors who were watched and controlled without exception, their cars included.

Few events were so viciously attacked with might and main – in the mass media, at public rallies and in political structures – as were the events in Međugorje. There was hardly a newspaper in Bosnia and Herzegovina and beyond as had not published a whole multitude of fabrications at the expense of the visionaries, priests and parishioners associating the events with "hostile" emigration, counterrevolution and anti-government activity.

In spite of the pressure exerted in various ways, the visionaries have been *unwavering* from the first day, remaining persistent in their statements about the *supernaturality of the event they had experienced*. Neither the doctors nor the priests, neither the rel-

107

atives nor the police or the authorities could confuse or break them.

The first few days, as it remained recorded, had been very important for a more tranquillised course later. Having overcome the fright of the first meeting, the children decided to go to the scene of the unusual event the next day, June 25. And what happened? *"All of a sudden a light flashed. And the children saw Our Lady, but without a child in her arms. She was indescribably beautiful, happy and smiling. And she beckoned them to come closer."* On the site of the apparition were **Mirjana Dragićević, Vicka Ivanković, Ivan Dragićević, Ivanka Ivanković, Marija Pavlović** and **Jakov Čolo**, the youngest of them. They prayed Our Father, Hail Mary and Glory Be with the Woman. After the conversation Our Lady promised to come the next day again. The rumour spread quickly about the village and its surroundings, and the next day many came to Bijakovići attracted by curious stories.

On the hill above the hamlet there would gather as many as several thousands of people, keeping vigil in prayer and song, and the children, not in fear any more, would convey the purport of their talks with Our Lady.

Many would take a handful of earth, a twig or two of bramble, pomegranate, sage and the like, especially pieces of stone, carrying all that as a sign of hope.

As early as on the third day of apparitions, appearing to Marija on her way downhill, for the second time that day, Our Lady said: "Peace, peace, peace, and only peace", and these words have become a symbol of the Međugorje apparitions. They have been spoken and conveyed numberless times in this parish and in the whole world, to all people regardless of faith, nation, race, political beliefs.

From that moment on hosts of people from the whole world have been coming to Međugorje and Bijakovići, even during the war, with their problems, sicknesses, anxieties... For, it is through personal and family peace that the peace in the world is achieved, says the Queen of Peace.

All who come – who find themselves in deep concentration and prayer in St James church, on the Hill of Apparitions, under the cross on Križevac – come actually in search of peace of their own heart: both the richest and the poorest, the healthy and the sick, those in top positions and those without any position.

"I am the Queen of Peace", said Our Lady to the visionaries during one of their meetings. Since that time the 25th of June has been consecrated to her. In the pre-war years as many as two hundred thousand pilgrims would gather for the day of the Queen of Peace, pressed in the crush of narrow streets, buses parked on the lawns and fields, between the houses and outside the village, cars with most different registration plates. Beside the Croatian language – in the stream of visitors, in groups reposing in the shade of the oak trees, in the church, on Podbrdo and on Križevac – one could hear, all day and night, English, German, Italian, Flemish, Spanish, Portuguese, Polish, French, Check, Hungarian, Slovak and other languages one had never heard here before. People of different cultures, customs, languages understand each other perfectly. Nobody inconveniences anybody.

Is there any human building, historical sight or natural beauty that would, like Međugorje in its fifteen years of apparitions, attract, considering the situation we are in, thousands of pilgrims dripping with "the sweat of their face" in the summer heat while visiting the church, Podbrdo and Križevac. Many of them, in spite of the most modern aircraft, need as many as 24 hours to reach their destination. On the other hand, a large number of them travel in buses two days and nights without rest.

The apparitions on Podbrdo, today known in the whole world as the Hill of Apparitions, lasted for six days. After that the authorities barred the access to that spot, both for the visionaries and the people, who had started coming in large numbers. At that time, at the suggestion of the parish priest, Father Jozo Zovko, who had been away on a journey when the apparitions started, the recitation of the rosary and after that the Mass celebration were transferred to the church. The parish priest himself was suspicious about the apparitions at first, but later in the media and, after his arrest, at court he was found guilty of having organised this "hostile propaganda" and sentenced to three years of imprisonment.

The local authorities, in agreement with state authorities, labelled the events as antisocialist and subversive, organised by the enemy. This especially applied to the persons that claimed to have seen a sign or an unusual phenomenon in the skies. The eye-witnesses from those times will testify even

110

today to many signs that appeared to the visionaries: motley small balloons, the figure of a woman under the cross on Križevac, the large letters MIR (peace) written in the sky, etc. Apart from many having been taken to the police for interrogation, where they were maltreated and heard over and over again, many people were sentenced to shorter terms of imprisonment summarily. Not even the children, who persistently and openly testified to their experiences, were let alone. They were repeatedly subjected to medical examinations and egged on to tell on the organisers for a big prize. The visionaries remained steadfast, however, claiming that what they were saying was truth. One of Our Lady's statements at that time was, "Let the people believe firmly and have no fear of anything".

It was not only the municipal authorities that were putting pressure on the visionaries, priests and the faithful. In the state-controlled newspapers the Međugorje events were mentioned on July 5, 1981 for the first time, when they were labelled as hostile and subversive. Articles, reports, and newspaper stories are probably going to find their place in the history of newspaper lies whose authors were competing in who would tell more lies. Reading these articles today, one gets the impression that for the authorities of the former Yugoslavia all evil of this world seemed to be originating in and coming from Međugorje. And the children, of whom the youngest was attending the fourth class of the primary school, according to these newspaper texts, were intent on subverting the state, so that in mid August special police forces came to the village with special equipment and trained dogs.

One cannot fully grasp the situation as it was fifteen years ago, all that repression and agitation in hot summer days, unless we recall at least some of the headlines published in the newspapers throughout Yugoslavia. Here they are: "'Our Lady' of Čitluk – commonplace superstition" (Večernje novine, 8.7.'81), "The Summer Festival of Čitluk" (Nedjeljna Dalmacija, 23.8.'81), "Our Lady of Čitluk Fizzled Out" (AS, 24.7.'81). The events were declared "Séances", "Superstition Fair", then the headlines like "Our Lady Has Been Launched", "The Ustasha Madonna", "Our Lady Invented by Clericalist-Nationalists", Our Lady was invented by "the enemies of our country disguised in long black cloaks" (Večernje novosti); the apparitions have been programmed "From a centre, by individuals in the Catholic hierarchy" (Oslobođenje), "who from their shelters in Mostar and Zagreb are trying to bring the people of the western Herzegovina back into 1941". The newspapers were backed, especially zealously, by the Sarajevo Television according to which Our Lady of Međugorje has emerged on the Mostar – Captol line, etc.

These articles always mention the name of the parish priest of Međugorje Fr. Jozo Zovko, eager to discover his "guilts" from the past in order to "prove" that he was the organiser of everything that was happening about the visionaries and Our Lady. No wonder that Fr. Jozo was arrested on August 17, 1981 on charges of "hostile propaganda" (Milan Vuković: Article 133 of Penal Code of

SFRY versus Međugorje, court persecution of Fr. Jozo Zovko). On the basis of a fabricated bill of indictment, by extracting quotations from his homilies, in spite of a multitude of registered witnesses of the defence who had not even been heard, Fr. Jozo was sentenced to three years of imprisonment in a typically Stalinist process. Of course, in the media it had first been "proved" that he was guilty, an at court his guilt was only "corroborated".

The visionaries, in spite of all pressures and threats, showed maturity and courage in the first days already, so that their meetings with Our Lady, after the visits to the Hill of Apparitions had been banned, reminded of the first Christian centuries: visions take place in groves, in tobacco fields, in houses, in vineyards – far from the eyes of the authorities.

The visionaries, still children, were conveying the messages which, in their simplicity, openness and hope, were appealing to every human heart no matter how reserved, self-sufficient, weak or proud it might be. It was just this appeal to conscience that spread the messages and made people from the farthest parts come to pray in a "village at the end of the world", where they were met with friendship and openheartedness of the people there.

Many a time it was asked, mainly without reason, "why in Međugorje" of all places, why has Our Lady not appeared here or there. The hidden meaning of this question suggests the attitude towards the people there, their nationality and history. The ideological pressures manifested themselves in most varied ways, and one of them is just this suspicious attitude. When I asked Fr. Slavko Barbarić, a priest who keeps contacts with pilgrims, who follows the messages and who is a witness of everything that is going on here, why Our Lady had chosen this parish, he replied, half jokingly: If she had chosen another place I am sure it would have to have a smaller hill (The Hill of Apparitions), a bigger hill (Križevac) and a church. And then added quite seriously: Our Lady said to the visionaries several times: 'I have chosen this parish in a special way and want to guide it. I keep it in love and want everybody to be mine', or 'For I (Our Lady) and my Son have a special plan with this parish'.

This plan is being realised into an integral shrine, in the triangle Podbrdo–Church–Križevac, for they are connected with many a step, prayer and vigil of the pilgrims. There is no pilgrim as does not visit all the three places, bearing deep in himself the feeling that all the three are connected and complement each other. Originally, the first place of apparitions, Podbrdo, is still a place of meetings with Our Lady, when in exceptional evening hours they bring people together for meditation and prayer. The mountain path has become worn out with the steps of many who have never before in their lifetime set foot on a rocky ground.

The huge concrete cross, built as a vow of the parishioners in memory of the 1933rd anniversary of Christ's death, on the hill of Šipovac, catches the eye from distance, and the first thing a pilgrim gets to see of Međugorje is the cross. For half a century

114

have the people of the parish been gathering round it, laying their troubles down at its foot, and today many come to its foot barefoot, climbing full of hope from one station to another of the Way of the Cross. On the first Sunday after the Nativity of Our Lady, in the September fragrance of sage and immortelle, there would gather more than three hundred thousand people for the Mass, and even during the war years the figure exceeded forty thousand.

The church – consecrated to St James the Apostle, who is also known as patron of pilgrims, whose old statue among the concelebrants gives the impression of a patriarch arrived from Biblical times – receives multitudes into its interior and surroundings every day. Masses in different languages, information, adorations, vigils, confessions. And nobody disturbs anybody, everything is in decent order and peace.

Today the shrine gives the impression of a gallery in the open air, where everything is in its place: stations, statues, pictures in the parish rooms, stained-glass windows.

Throngs of people during feasts, different languages, races and costumes make a mosaic put together, with human help, by a divine hand. And from the hill-side above Čitluk, from where one gets the best view of them, Međugorje and Bijakovići with their hamlets seem like an extended ring of houses and light, cut in two by the line running from the small bridge, past the church and further towards Križevac.

Inside this circle a mystery occurs that attracts

streams of pilgrims. The main messages, during all these years, are: prayer, conversion, fasting, penance, peace.

As early as on the third day of the apparitions Our Lady urged: "Peace, peace, peace – and only peace", and later she would often speak of the need for peace, its being threatened, and the sufferings that menace people with its loss. Other messages are also in the service of peace and salvation; without their implementation peace cannot be achieved. The simplicity of the messages shows the love that Our Lady expresses through them for the visionaries and for all people who are ready to accept them. In order to understand their simplicity it is enough to read only a few messages:

"Dear children! I have already told you that I have chosen you in a special way, being what you are. I, your Mother, love you all. And in every difficult moment have no fear! For I love you even when you are far from me and my Son. Do not let, I implore you, my heart shed the tears of blood for the souls dying in sin. Therefore, dear children, pray, pray, pray! Thank you for having responded to my call!" (May 24, 1984)

"Dear children! God wants to make you holy. That is why He is calling you through me to a complete surrender. Let the Holy Mass be your life. Understand that the church is a palace of God, a place where I bring you together to show you the way to God. Come and pray, do not watch others nor gossip them but rather let you life be a testimony on the way of holiness. Churches deserve respect and are consecrated. For God who became man dwells in them day and night. So, my little ones, have faith and pray that the Father may multiply your faith, and then ask for whatever you need. I am with you. I rejoice at your conversion and shelter you with my motherly mantle. Thank you for having responded to my call!" (April 25, 1988)

"Dear children! Today I am calling upon all of you, who have heard my message of peace, to put it, with seriousness and love, into your life. Many are those who think that they are doing much by talking about the messages but do not live them. I, dear children, call you to life and to change everything that is negative in you so that it may turn into the positive and into life. Dear children, I am with you and I would like to help each of you live the glad tiding. I am here, dear children, to help you and to bring you to heaven. There is joy in heaven by which you can start living it already. Thank you for having responded to my call!" (May 25, 1991)

"Dear children! Today I am calling you to conversion. It is the most important message I have given here. My little ones, I want each of you to be the bearer of my messages. I invite you, my little ones, to live the messages I have been giving you all these years. This time is a time of grace. Especially now when the Church is calling you to prayer and conversion. I, too, my little ones, am calling you to live my messages I have given you during this time since I have been appearing here. Thank you for having responded to my call!" (February 25, 1996)

The war and the aggression suffered by the Croatian people reduced the number of pilgrims to Međugorje, but not for a single day has Međugorje remained without pilgrims, in spite of the heaviest war afflictions in its neighbourhood. Many who had put off their coming, or had been about to come here for the first time, went on living the messages of the Queen of Peace in their countries through prayer groups, acts of charity for the war victims, influencing the public opinion in their midst so that people may learn the real truth about the aggressor and the victim.

Both in war and peace Međugorje has helped a large number of people all over the world to embrace their faith again, and these same people have, through Međugorje, helped the Croatian people in their hardest times. No wonder, therefore, that many have proved wrong in their anticipations that Međugorje, as a result of war, will be "forgotten" and that the pilgrims will "grow cool". Again the stream of pilgrims, in prayer and hope, is flowing towards Podbrdo, Križevac and the St James', whole-heartedly living the time of grace, as the Queen of Peace once called it, not letting this time go past them.

Table of Contents